SHERWIN WASHINGTON

3D

THE POWER OF YOUR SPIRIT VS THE IMAGES IN YOUR MIND

CONTENTS

3D

INTRODUCTION
Your Break Through

My palms are starting to sweat; my heart rate rises as I step towards the flamming stack of bricks. I paced back n forth, taking deep breaths while focusing on the orange flares from the center floor. My ears are attentive to the cheers of people around, but I'm trying to decipher the voice of my parents. I glance to the side of the mat, and I don't see them. I thought to myself, where could they be? Mannnn... I've trained really hard to get to this point. The convention was full, but I spotted my parents in each other's faces towards a side door. I immediately rush towards them, wanting to explain that it's my time to perform on the floor. As I got closer, I overheard my father saying; *"Well, raise him then,"* as he opened the door.

My mother shouted aggressively, *"he's going to need you,"* as the door shut behind him. Standing in confusion, I heard a voice behind me saying, C'mon, son; you're up next! One of the judges grabbed my hand and escorted me back to the floor. As I stepped back on the mat, I couldn't help but glance back n forth at that side door and the flames burning ahead of me. Tears started to drop as I approached the stack. I glanced at the seating area, where my mom watched me in distress. I looked at the glow from the judge's table where the trophies sat and another look at the bricks in front of me as I approached! I immediately tightened my belt, took some last deep breaths, and just broke out crying in the middle of the floor!

As a child, I just knew I was born to fight. The Images I watched in movies molded my mind to become what I saw. Seeing one good guy defeat an army of opponents always seems exciting. I wanted to experience all the action live, so I begged my mom to sign me up for Martial Arts lessons. Throughout my experiences, it was a lot of valuable lessons to learn in this new world of fighting. For instance, most kids get excited about dressing in uniforms with different colored belts around their waste. But as an adult now, I've learned that these colors represented levels of the mind. You see, martial arts is not all about fighting. It's really about defending, self-control, and confidence. It's about training your mind to focus all your energy on what's right in front of you. In other words, your power is in your focus, but if I can distract, intimidate, or conflict you as an enemy, you've already lost a battle before the fight even begun. Brick breaking is a perfect example. Have you ever watched any martial arts competitions and felt the pain of fighters smashing their fists through a stack of bricks? Is it real or make-believe?... Well, it's definitely real if done correctly. You see, it's all in the technique.

Training your mind and body to become one in itself. Visualizing the break going through, keeping your muscles tense, deep breathing, focusing all your energy inside, and dropping your body weight down through the center of bricks with your hand. In other words, it's about focus and execution. Any other conflicts and you will be successful at just breaking bones. This also applies to fighting opponents even if the opponents are not physically inside a ring. You see, your opponents in life can be the bricks in your way that you've prayed for God to remove. But sometimes God's answers don't look like the prayers you requested. God has an answer for you, but you may not see it because you see life in 3D. Here's what I mean,

I'm writing to you from the inside, but I also have bricks that stand in my way. My prayers were always to be set free, but I still waited awhile for my answers. It's like every other morning when I awake; I can remember the dreams I've been having at night of me being back at my home. It's the freedom I have been praying for because of the loneliness here. For a while now, I've been feeling angry and depressed, and abandoned at the same time. Thoughts are always rehearsed in my mind of the event that landed me in 1st place. I'll share some of what I'm talking about, and you will understand me more.

It was a Friday evening, and my mom pulled up in our driveway. We noticed a van parked out front. *"It's the cableman,"* my mom said. As we approached our front door, he greeted us on how our day was going. Nothing is out of the ordinary to me. But I did notice him holding a concealed bag in his hand. 20 minutes later, flashes came down the hallways, and my mom realized what he was in the house for. He wanted to snap pictures in the house without my mother's consent. She quickly confronted him, and things escalated. This was the only time I witnessed my mom slapped by a man and running off crying. So what does an innocent child do in this situation? With no other witnesses around, I stood there loading up with anger and fear as my eyes locked onto him like a target. But quickly in my thoughts, I glanced across my side and remembered my father's abandonment. I looked across the room where my mom was on the phone, crying and now distressed. So I now stand with two options, face my opponent or run for cover. I've been competing for a while now, but the fight became real. I was up next! What stood before me now were flaming bricks that needed to be broken. My next move is the reason I'm writing to you now. These burning bricks were my inner desire to fight, but I could not break the Image I'd just witnessed. The intimidation of him and the background crying disrupted my focus, and I cried loudly and chose to run. This traumatic experience built this wall around my mind, and now this little boy sits inside an adult body, praying to be set free.

This book is based on my personal stories, and it shows how our Spiritual Father revealed the power in me to defeat the Images that held control over me. It was birthed through a verse in the Bible. Mark 9:21 reads; And Jesus asked his father, How long ago was this happening to him? And the father said, since childhood! You see, God was answering my prayers all along. But I couldn't see it because my sight was always in 3D. The dreams I consistently had of my childhood home were the root cause of the mental bricks in my adult life. The fears of men, abandonment, and failure were all rooted in one incident from the past. Most of the time, your fight in this life comes from the Images you've experienced back then and have you bound in your mind now. You've been praying for God to help you remove these bricks; he inspired me to write this for you. Throughout this book, you will see how invisible Images are built and how you can activate your power to break them. It takes focus and execution to be free, and that little boy/girl inside you is the one that has to break through.

CHAPTER ONE
Your Colors vs. Your Image

Power:

The ability to direct or influence the behavior of others or the course of events.

Image:

(noun) represents the external form of a person or thing in art.

Fight:

(noun) a violent confrontation or struggle.

My hands started to tense while gripping my armrest. My eardrums rattled from the increased soundwaves as she tiptoed down the hallway. A shadow reflected from the ground in her peripheral, and she immediately turned and hollered. The usual tripping on your own feet while running expectation happened next. But the unexpected happened to me as this man approached and stood over her. Breathing heavily, she raised her arms, begging for mercy, and the scene rolled around to the barrel of his shotgun, jumping off the screen, pointing directly in my face. I ducked and tossed the shades immediately, glancing around to see who else was quietly laughing. Watching a film is more exciting to me when seen in 3D. These films are motion pictures made to give an illusion of three-dimensional solidity, usually with the help of special glasses worn by us viewers. To see the effects of a three-dimensional image, you must understand how it works. This unique lens shows two pictures simultaneously—one to each eye. One part of the picture is in red, and the other is in blue. One eye will see only the red part; one eye will see the blue part. By splitting the picture into two different colors and wearing the two different colored lenses, you now have two different images coming to the two individual eyes. Now the brain gets tricked by receiving two different perceptions, which interpret this such as we see in 3-D.

I can admit to having some passion for darker films because I get excited about where the light is eventually shown. Movies are all about the lights, the camera, and the actions, much like today's life. Films and life have a common goal; to make deposits in your mind so that you can *get the picture.* It gets a lot more interesting when we experience it in three dimensions. The world always shows us a dark picture in motion, but the light always shines by exposing the illusion behind what we see. A quick example I'll use is My Bloody Valentine 3D. A horror film that was released in 2009. In a brief synopsis, it's about an inexperienced coal miner named Tom Hanniger who caused an accident that killed five men and put the 6th man 'Harry,' into a coma. A year later, Harry woke up and murdered 22 people with a pickaxe before being killed himself. 10 years later, Tom returned to that same hometown but still was haunted by those past events. The film introduces the pickaxe-wielding killer again dressed with a miner's mask returning for unfinished killing business. Tom now was thinking, is this just the ghost of Harry returning in the illusion of his memories, or was it him that came to claim more lives? As a viewer, I realized the real problem was experiencing hallucinations of his split personalities. In other words, he was now experiencing his life in 3D. The image he saw because of his hallucinations was so powerful that he began to fight and kill the people. He reacted to everybody he felt threatened by. On the flip side, as I watched, I reacted to the powerful images I was receiving. 3d Images of thrown pickaxes flying off the screen, fireball explosions blowing off the screen, and every special effect you can think of caused a reaction in me. I was in the middle of a fight about what seemed natural and what was not.

With this experience, I learned that my brain was being tricked by the perceptions I received. Now With all of that being said, let me give you a personal examination with a few questions.

The last time you had the condition of your eyes checked was when? Right now, how do you see America?............. Think about the two different colors America represent during voting seasons on the map screens.............. Red and blue should look familiar, right?....... That's obvious, but if I were to post a picture of a human eyeball on a screen and say to you that this eyeball now represents America, what colors can you see in this picture now?...... I'd say you see black and white correct?....... Predominantly white and a little circle of black, to be exact. You see, it's a difference between the colors we see vs. the image we perceive; it all just depends on the condition of the eye.

Let me go deeper. For example, in the eye of the *"dominate whites,"* the blacks are perceived as ghetto or more violent. They're perceived to speak aggressively and threateningly. They are more prone to be just a worker ant from a ghetto and not business owners with credit issues. In the eye of the "circle of blacks," the whites are perceived as wealthy and usually have the best credit. They usually speak proper English *"(talk white)."* They're perceived to own assets and may have the best education. Both eyes are conditioned to see the picture one way, but the problem is not the eye. It's the image being perceived. With that being said, is the image you're presenting based on a color that people see?...... I love to use metaphors to teach principles, so let's look at this in more ways. If you look in a person's eyes, you may not only see black and white. The eyes can come in different shades of color. Some people may view the world in clarity through contact lenses instead of glasses. But the color in their eye is what you usually see. So if you don't mind me asking, what color do you have eyes for when choosing your mates?...... Do you prefer an area outside of your shade? Specifically, in the black community, it's usually categories of colors. This means that red, yellow, brown, and black are all considered to be like African Americans. So do you usually choose a color based on some of the stereotypes? In other words, Do you prefer tall, dark, and handsome? Are all the blackberries sweet to you, or do you like the attitude that comes with that body shape? Do you choose yellow and red because it seems to be the finest artwork? Or is the white preferred because of security and a yes ma'am on your side? Are brown and tan preferred because they seem to be the hardest workers for your team? My point is its different characteristics and cliches in this world, and society can trick the mind and allow you to see the picture one way. But it's only because you allow it. The world wants you to see the dominant images based on the colors, but my question is, does your image fit in the lines of your shaded area, or does your image stand out from it? Not all white men bring security to relationships, and they are some white women who are very dramatic with men. Not all black men are tall and come with a total package, and not all black women have nasty attitudes. The reds and the light skins are not always the better choice; they're a lot of beautiful black and brown vixens to choose from. Not all blacks are poor with challenged credit, and not all whites are rich and wealthy. There are a lot of blacks who speak proper English and have excellent educations, and there are a lot of whites who collect food stamps and use government assistance.

My point is, does the color matter most, or does the image matter most? You have two eyes debating over one picture to judge the clarity of what's being seen, but the images matter most. The Image always holds the power, and whoever is in control of the image has that power. Think of it this way: if you constantly show me a particular behavior and attitude or carry yourself a certain way, you're conditioning my eye to see you in one way. But that behavior may not be the truth about who you are. Attitudes and behaviors are your state of the mindset adopted by the environment you grew around, but now you show split personalities in the eyes around you. So who's in control of your image, and what state of mind are you living in? Like the voting season metaphor, your state is powered by the red or the blue. People have the option to vote and choose any side. They both have a particular way of thinking and how they perceive the way society should be run. When it's all said and done, a leader becomes in a position of power to represent that state, and his decisions govern everyone. How do you see and represent yourself? Have you adopted the mindset and presented an image the culture only wants to show the world? You have options to vote on yourself and choose to follow the best representation of yourself.

As I briefly explained how 3-D images work, I wanted you to 1st see and understand your life and the resemblance to what we experience within films. And the second thing is how we are divided by our colors and how society wants us to split our minds up with confusion and illusions of who we are. Some of us are walking around with these split personalities because we can't decide which image is real. We're living in 3D with the whole world seeing through the lens of red and blue or black and white. It's always a fight and struggles on what's being perceived and what's being shown, and we kill each other as a result of it. They're making the color bigger than the image, but without both eyes seeing together, there is no bigger image. It's just a one-sided picture. Before we dive deeper into these chapters, I wanted you and I to learn to see past the color and put some focus on your Image. If you view the world through the lens of your color, then toss that to the side, rise, and look around. Don't continue in this fight with colors because your image will always be bigger than your color.

CHAPTER TWO
Imagine Your Reality

I had a firm grip on the metal bar above my kneecaps while waiting in amazement at my surroundings. Everything seemed real as I looked up, down, and around me. Immediately I was jerked as we started moving towards this huge mountain climb. The seats vibrated with every click of clack sound while my face pointed towards these clouds. The rising clicks continued until I finally reached the horizon. As I began to fall, my guts dropped below my feet, and I began to tense up while I looped around these vast hills. I was in and out of tunnels, up and down hills, and finally, I circled back to the starting point. I could hear the snickering as I unbuckled and removed my headset. I immediately shoved the headset in the hands of the next child in line and walked off with my mom toward the food court. I had mixed emotions about this scary but exciting experience. I pondered how something could feel so real but not genuine.

I want to show you the difference between the life you've been living and what's reality. As we journey throughout life, we hit many milestones along the way. Specifically, the timeframe of childhood to adulthood is what I'm referring to. Depending on your age, consider the significant birthday milestones like sweet sixteens, the legal 21s, the dirty 30s, and so on. At every milestone, you can remember what happened before and after those times. But at what point in your life did you stop and realize reality? At 18, you had to leave the nest. After you finish school, you hear the *"welcome to the real-life"* voices of the world. Do you remember how anxious you were while waiting in that long line of 21 and up? And now you've found yourself sitting in this seat of adult and parenthood and forgot what you thought reality looked like? You started to feel the effects of a roller coaster of bills coming down faster than your income going up. The heartbreaking thrills and chills of relationships going in, out, and looping around in the depths of your heart. And how about these kids of ours? How we start off the morning with a fresh, clean house but reevaluate at the end of the day with a mess. I'm specifically talking about my children with that statement, but you get my point. Have you ever thought about how did you go from being a child that was full of joy and excitement, Anxiously waiting in that adventurous line of life and the skies were never a limitation to you, to now being dropped and you found yourself full of motion sickness on what you now see as reality? That motion sickness is what you feel every morning if your first thoughts are I'm sick of this. I'm sick of waking up every day and going through these motions of life. I'm sick of these limitations and what to do or where to go. I'm sick of barely living decently without paying uncle sam and these recurring bills 1st. Whoever engineered this coaster of life needs to shut it down because I'm ready to get off this ride. Now does this virtually sound like your reality? If it does, let me teach you something I've learned about reality and where I'm going with all of this. It's a disconnection going on between your realities. For starters, in a virtual simulator, motion sickness is caused by too much virtual reality triggering your brain to make it think it's moving, but your body isn't. It creates a disconnect between the two that confuses to make you feel sick. Virtual reality is a computer-generated environment with senses and objects that appear real, immersing you in the surroundings through a headset. It's a simulated experience that employs pose tracking and 3D near-eyed displays to give you an immersive feel of a virtual world. That said, the headset you wear represents the mindset of how you view your reality. And It's a power struggle in your mind competing for complete control of this reality.

A perfect example comes from what you watch on TV...... I love the series on Netflix called the squid games. It became one of my favorites. It's about hundreds of desperate, money-trapped people who are invited to compete in a series of children's games. If they win, they will walk away with billions of dollars. But they must find out every game has a twist and deadly consequences. Most wouldn't make it out alive. One of these particular games is the game of tug of war. It's an example I want to use that consists of two teams playing tug of war across two raised platforms. The goal was for the opponents to pull each other off the platform resulting in the opposing team falling to their deaths. I said all that to say A tug of war game is going on inside your mind. And it's like a game that's taken place in the arena of your imagination. Please take some notes and review your imagination to see how it works from the inside.

Picture us taking steps on top of your nose towards the double curtains of your eyes. And as we step through, you will see a sign on the right that reads: Welcome to the arena where all the action of forming new ideas, images, and concepts of external objects not present to the senses takes place. But here's what I want to do. I want you to see a new sign I printed for us. My sign reads: Welcome to the place where the words Imagine, and Nation are divided. You see, your imagination reflects two parts of you, and it's pulled in two directions by the power of people. Jot down these notes. The people represent the nations and the power struggle between them. But I want us to locate something as we walk through your arena...

As we look forward, that shiny object is your own risen platform. It was built by a man named Justus Von Liebig. Another term for this platform is called the *"looking glass"* or, in better terms, the "mirror." The mirror is the familiar battleground I, you, and everybody else are never exempt from. Every day you meet on this specific platform that reflects your appearance and the environment outside of you. This is what I like to call the physical battleground. Now I want to point out some things while we're in here. What you can see physically is only some of what is reflected. If you look closely, you can see who's really telling you to live in those conditions. You can see who's telling you to dress that way. You can see who was telling you to raise your kids that way. I told you no one is exempt. The reflection battle is still the same whether you have a newborn or a toddler. The battles are just bouncing off of you for now. The environment outside you shows me the culture you're in. It shows where you reside and the philosophies taught in that environment. This is the source of the power struggle inside your arena. And I'll begin to prove it to you as we get outside of your curtains.

I have a few verses I want to teach from. The 1st one is found in the book of 2 Corinthians 10:4-5. It reads: *"For the weapons of our warfare are not carnal, but mighty through God to pulling down strongholds; Casting down Imaginations, and every high thing that exalts itself against the knowledge of God, and bringing into captivity every thought to the obedience of Christ."* The word *"imagination"* in the Bible means internal arguments of the mind. It's a yelling match of false arguments within yourself. The Bible defines strongholds as powerful arguments, philosophies, and doubts pulling against the other wills and beliefs but also arguments against God. The majority of the time, yielding to other belief systems against yours is because of fear. In your imagination, you fear(respect) more of anyone who seems to have a position of power, which is your life's controlling factor. God wants me to show that your imagination is so powerful that even the world uses it against you. For good and for evil purposes. Here's another verse to glance at. Genesis 11:6 reads: *"And the Lord said, Behold, the people is one, and they have all one language; and this they begin to do: and now nothing will be restrained from them, which they have imagined doing."* This is the story of the Tower of Babel, where the people came together to build their city with a tower to reach the heavens.

In the days of Noah after the flood, God's plans were still the same as at the beginning of creation. His desire was for his people to be fruitful and to multiply and for the people to fill the earth. They were supposed to scatter and fill the earth in different regions, but something shifted the people from obeying his purpose. That shift came from an influential person name Nimrod. Nimrod is 1st mentioned in Genesis 10 from the family line of Noah. Cush was his dad, and he was the first great warrior on earth after the flood. Just a note, the Bible described giants being in the land before the flood, and Nimrod was considered the first to appear afterward.

Nimrod was also the best hunter in the world. It is written that he was a great hunter before God. Nimrod also built and controlled his kingdoms of Babel, Erech, Accad, and Calneh, in the land of Shinar, where the tower was. He had influential power over the people because they feared his reputation as their time's best warrior and killer. Just think about that, one man is powerful enough to destroy a grizzly bear, so how do people look in his eyes? It's easy to see where the control factor is coming from, but this is one example to show the evil side of how the imagination can be used. Commentators said that Nimrod, who became prideful, wanted to construct his tower high enough so God could not kill everyone with the flood again. That sounds like some of what our modern-day scientist tries to prove. But God already promised his ancestor not to flood out humanity again, but I guess he didn't get the memo. So what does anybody in a position of power do to accomplish their hidden agenda? They use the people. The scripture says, *"and it came to pass, as they journeyed from the east, that they found a plain in the land of Shinar. They use brick for stone and slime for mortar. And they said, let us build a city and a tower to reach heaven and make a name for ourselves unless we are scattered all over the face of the earth."* (Gen 11:2-4).

The people were headed in the right direction of life. They were headed east, representing where the sun rises, but they stopped and turned to the west, where the sun sets. The people turned and headed towards darkness to build a name for themselves, which you know is a source of pride. Take this moment to think about the way you've been living and why you live that way. Are you walking towards the east or the west? If your direction is west, consider who you're following and why. One man controlled the decision of a group of people because they imagined what he could do to them if they rebelled against his authority. And we see the results; they rebelled against God and decided that another *"man"* knows what's best for their life. The scripture calls it the tower of Babel, but I view it as a tower of pride. It reflects the hearts of people in the world, with positions of power that are using you to build up something for their namesake. It's easy to understand why God destroyed the earth by the flood the first time. God mentions the power of your imagination in Genesis 6:5: And God saw that the wickedness of man was great in the earth and that every *"Imagination"* of the thoughts of his heart was only evil continually. Again, the people were headed west in the wrong direction, and this represents you and the evil side in the arena of your imagination.

Now I want to introduce you to another example by the name of Walter Elias Disney. Walt was an American animator, film producer, and entrepreneur. I'm bringing your attention to him because Walt demonstrated his imagination's power for people's practical purposes. A little history lesson about Walt: he tapped into the power of his imagination as he grew interested in drawing. At age 7, his entrepreneurial spirit kicked in as he sold his first sketches to his neighbors. He found a career in Kansas City as an advertising cartoonist in his young adult years, and best known for creating mickey mouse, created in 1928 as a silent cartoon.

During the Great Depression, Walt birthed and produced snow white and the 7 Dwarfs at $1.4 million. And you thought your life was depressing; look what he accomplished in the middle of great depressing times. But here's the best part, in his imagination, Walt was inspired to advance in the entertainment of motion pictures to provide for the public needs of the people. He decided to purchase land in Florida to build his world of what we now know as Disney World. Now doesn't that sound familiar to Nimrod's story? One man, one imagination, and a desire to build something for the people and not use the people to build something for himself. You see, he touched the hearts, minds, and emotions of millions worldwide from experience in one location. Instead of pride, he built happiness and joy and a universal means of communication with the people of every nation. Look at it this way, when you travel to the east of the United States, it will cost you about $100 a ticket to walk inside Walt's arena. Now take a moment and think about what I just said. It costs you $100 to walk past his curtains and experience the inside of his mind!...... But how does all this relate to you?..... Well, as you look in the mirror again, I wanted you to see that it's a Nimrod and a Walt inside your imagination. The two reflections on the platform represent them and have power. There is no limitation on either side. If you're confused and have questions about the power struggle inside you, then stop and check out the two nations.

The answer is always inside the conflict, and here it is: To have control and power in your life, you have to get all your internal arguments on one accord. In other words, both nations have to come together in your arena for you to do impossible things to change what's outside your curtains. The scattered nation demonstrated that power at the tower of Babel, but it was for an evil purpose. You have the power in your imagination to live differently and to do impossible things for good purposes. God proves it in his word already, so don't allow the intimidations of others to convince you otherwise. Disney didn't allow it, and he used it for good purposes.

The Bible is real, but some people in the nation live virtually. They battle within themselves on what's real for them or not. But God shows us other ways to view our reality. It's incredible how God came down, saw them come together at the tower, and said, *"Nothing will stop them when they come together as one, so I will confuse their language when they try communicating with each other."* That may explain our different languages today, but God wanted me to focus on another way of looking at that verse. In my reality, I once decided to build my own business in one location, but God allowed my internal language to be confused so that these books would scatter around the earth. The purpose was to fill the nations on the earth, not to build something for me. More on this later, but I said that because you have a choice about your reality. I wanted to end this chapter by saying, *"This book costs you very little to walk inside my arena, but what's the price for me to walk through yours? How big is your imagination?"* Reread this chapter and put this book down until tomorrow. Think about this and Imagine the cost to your mind.

CHAPTER THREE
Know Love and Know Power

In our society of social media today, platforms such as Facebook have anniversary reminders that capture the time and place of recent thoughts and pictures. The media has become a great digital photo album, but it mostly only captures what we want the world to see. Let's say you see an old classmate or someone you knew in the past that posts a lot of selfies. The majority of the time, it's the background surroundings that they're advertising for you. Their genuine interest in informing you about how well they're doing now. The likes and followers they're trying to accumulate are usually for self-gratification purposes. I know this to be true because I was one of them. I wanted to keep up with the media world and advertise unrealistic happiness. The memory bank of the media made me reflect on what's behind my smile. Just think about your parents' old photos of you as a child. The picture day photos of you in the school yearbooks or some old vacations you took when you were young. Do you remember when they made you say *"cheese"* a few times? But as time grew, things began to happen, and you started experiencing life that shifted your inside smile. As I got older, I noticed my photo album shifted from smiles to frowns. The picture album began to look like mugshots but without a crime. Flipping through the album from childhood to young adult pictures showed a progression of anger. The older I got, the angrier I became. Something painful was hidden, so I started digging for some truths.

Please take pictures of yourself and ponder where or who you were with. How were you feeling at that moment? Do you have any pictures of you forcing a smile, but you weren't happy inside? Yeah, I'm talking about the picture's you're not being honest about. I'm sure you've heard plenty of times that a picture freezes time for us. It captures the moment of emotions and the era you were living in, and by now, you know my focus is all on that background. It's what happened behind you despite what's trying to be shown in the picture. In other words, the part of the captured scene furthest from view is what's hurting you. But that's ok now because I'm here to go deeper with those pictures. So 1st, I want you to realize that you're a chosen disciple of God, and he has strolled through a few of your selfies. He's seen everything you went through then, what you're going through now, and what you will get through later. Yes, he knows you that well, and he knows the pain behind every faulty smile. For starters, I didn't think God understood me as well as I thought, so one day, I decided to open my pictures of where I was in my life and be honest with him. I said things like; You see God, in this picture, I was feeling myself; I had a little money in my account, so I treated myself to buy all those cubic zirconias around my neck. I was drinking a bit with this one, but I was only celebrating with my boys.....Anddddd. I didn't care about myself in this picture, but I just forced that smile as I stood behind them. As I tried to swipe on, his spirit said, *"Go back to that previous picture and stop there"!* Do you know God completely disregards every other picture except this particular one? God noticed something missing with that background, and we started concentrating on what I wanted to skip over.

Going back to the story of Mark, chapter 9 is where I want to give you a deeper understanding of what's going on. Verse 16 starts to read like this: *"Why are you arguing?"* He asked. A man in the crowd answered, Jesus, I brought you my son, possessed by a spirit that has robbed him of speech. Whenever it seizes him, it throws him to the ground. He foams at the mouth, gnashes his teeth, and becomes rigid. I asked your disciples to drive out the spirit, but they couldn't. *"You unbelieving generation,"* Jesus replied, how long shall I stay with you? How long shall I put up with you? Bring the boy to me. So they brought him. When the spirit saw Jesus, it immediately convulsed the boy. He fell to the ground and rolled around, foaming at the mouth. Jesus asked the boy's father. *"How long has he been like this?"* From childhood, he responded. This scene is captured in time for us to see something wrong with this picture.

This whole chapter is like a snapshot that shows a massive mountain in a blurry background, a crowd of people in a circle pointing fingers, disciples standing in faces of confusion, Jesus and a father looking downwards, and a little boy with his eyes rolled to the back with spit foam from his mouth. In this scene, I want to focus on their facial expression because it tells us more about them at the time. I'm sure you've heard the phrase, *"Stop living in the past."* Well, you're not living in the past; you're just stuck in the past. You're stuck in a place of solid feelings and reacting to life based on those feelings. Your dominant facial expressions show a mask or a truth of what you feel inside. Others may think you're mean because you always walk around with a frown, but you don't recognize that until you scroll and see yourself in pictures. Mine expressed unhappiness and unfulfillment, but yours may be different. You can notice your face by noticing your body's responses to life. You may be grown, but your attitude and behaviors are responding like a child. You're almost 50 and still think high schoolers are attracted to you. Or your automatic response to rules is they don't apply to you. You always want special treatment, and your face is stuck in entitlements. You may think my parents had better expectations of my behavior, but the problem must be added to your background.

In this story, the disciples of Jesus were expected to handle this matter a little more maturely than expected. The lights and power were shut off when the world showed up to the children of God. People in the world show up on the scene to approach *"church folks,"* expecting healing and deliverance, but they can't find any. Their powerlessness and faces show us that they knew something was wrong and missed something from way back. Before the stuck faces, I pointed out to you the blurry mountains. This is important because this background is the reason for their powerlessness. Jesus chose 12 disciples to follow him around as he taught about the Kingdom of Heaven. But as they traveled around with him, he stopped and said to them, some of you standing here will not taste death before you see the Kingdom of God coming with power. Not knowing what he meant, Jesus took three disciples and led them up a high mountain. Look at it as his inner circle going up with him. While up on this mountain, Jesus transfigured right before their eyes. They experienced the real power and glory of who God was. Up there is where they had a glimpse of where the source of light comes from. The man who always walked and talked with us is now here from heaven. Their eyes opened to who their birth parent was in life and who was always in charge. Their superhero, provider, protector, and head of all households were shown to them in great power—something they couldn't see from the bottom view.

Being on top of the world next to a spiritual parent reminds me of being next to our earthly parents. Where I am now is not where I have always been. My blurry background consists of an inner circle of my mom and me. The scripture said the disciples could hear the rumbling voice of God saying, *"This is my Son whom I love"* on top of that mountain. It was no different with me, as my mom probably rumbled the same words as I entered this world. And despite anything you went through, I'm confident your newborn ears heard the same rumbles of words from your parents. Everyone loves new life in the beginning; it's just your memory is blurred to that now. But being with momma was like being on top of the world. She was my light in this dark world. She was my leader, provider, protector, and the only Image I had of what love was supposed to look like. Examining how she moved in life was inspiring to know this is how God designed women to operate. My belly stayed full with that good ole country cooking throughout the weekdays and not just Sundays. I'm talking about rice and gravy with some cornbread muffins. Collard greens and neck bones. Maybe a little smoother porkchop or fried gizzards with a scoop of macaroni to the side. And I can't forget that Kool-Aid with extra sugar that's shaken and not stirred. The red flavor, to be exact, not cherry or strawberry but the red flavor! Being on the mountain had its days that I loved, but it also came with some corrections. Mama wasn't shy to introduce me to her belt to help keep me inside my boundaries. The same boundaries God had to remind them on that mountain by revealing who has real authority around here. But I'm talking old-school parenting, where I learn the meaning of respect with her in the house and the public eye. And note as a quick reminder what you learn will always be tested. For some strange reason, the test always seemed to show up when what was behind me always tried to show out............I dressed that up so you could get what I wanted to say, but let's continue. Mama always made me feel like we were on top of the mountain despite the economic status disguised in the valley. Loading dirty clothes in portable carts to walk in the cold to bus stops and catching transits back n forth to grocery stores never felt like a struggle. I loved following my leader around as I explored my little world. To me, status didn't matter when my room was full of toys to play with all the time. As long as the rest of the house didn't resemble a jungle gym, my face was full of smiles. She was the head of the household and ensured her head stayed straight by staying involved within the house of God. I followed her everywhere, including the church. My childhood church is one I could never forget. I watched my mom release her vocal talents in the church choir but secretly cried as she bowed her head in prayer. I didn't fully understand the deal but I was having a ball. I had church friends that felt like brothers and sisters to me. I remember easter plays and speeches we had to perform in front of the crowds of people who mostly showed up to the annual *"Jesus Ball."* Im being funny, but this was something to look forward to in my eyes.

Every year I had a different color suit I could pick to wear that Mama made sure I had. Except for the red one. That was my favorite color, but she never allowed that color for some reason. And speaking of clothes to wear, Mama made sure I at least had some new clothes twice a year. The beginning of the school year and the beginning of the New Year after Christmas break. It wasn't much, but I was thankful and felt good for the first week of school. She also kept me in line when it came to school as well. These early childhood years made me discover a little more about myself. I could remember winning a first-grade poster contest that captured pictures of me and the crash dummies for the news. It was an art contest about wearing seatbelts n stuff. No big deal; I just enjoyed drawing and showing Mama the pictures. I also won third place in the spelling bee contest and treasured that trophy to sit on our t.v. for another decoration in the house. Yeah, I had some *success* in elementary, but by the time I reached High School, I didn't ask any more questions about school anymore. I wanted to share a little blurred information about my adolescent mountain-top experiences. But mountain memories are just what they are. It's a memory of an experience that meant something to you back then. But you know, eventually, you have to come down. Peter struggled with that reality on top of the mountain. He was so awed that he suggested to Jesus that they should build houses for everyone to stay up there. He wanted to make an experience with this inner circle a permanent place to live in. He wanted to forget where he came from, which was at the bottom.

After God revealed to them the glory and splendor of who Jesus was, the atmosphere began to clear, and Jesus was the last man standing. He told them to remember this event and only speak about it after his death and resurrection. Their time came for them to head back down to the reality of the world. I understand your feelings, Peter, because I wanted to stay in that space forever. The atmosphere of feeling protected from the world below and the space of just us building on top of the world. Well, as time progressed, things began to shift on the way down.

Jesus and his inner circle came down and were immediately met by the world's problems. As they approached the other disciples(the outer circle), they saw a huge crowd around them and other religious scholars cross-examining them. As soon as the people in the crowd saw Jesus, they ran towards him, overjoyed as Jesus asked, what's the deal here? These other disciples were in a situation where they couldn't defend themselves. They were face to face with a battle they were supposed to handle but couldn't. And to make things worse, they had the eyes of the world watching and religious folks criticizing them. The same situation applied when I was faced with my introduction altercation. I became face to face with a battle that I couldn't handle. I felt the frustration these other disciples felt. And I noticed they couldn't defend themselves because their leader was gone. Remember now, he decided to choose his inner circle and left the rest behind to defend themselves against the world. When I read this, I thought, what made them so special, God? I immediately put myself in their shoes and said, God, why did you leave me? I did all this following and training, and I'm left here with these bricks of life in front of me. What made the others so special? Why do I feel so defenseless in life situations? I looked and didn't see my leader by my side either. Now do these types of questions arise inside of you as well? Do you feel some way because you think your other siblings or family members were treated better than you?..... But I started to notice something else about this picture. It was 12 disciples, and Jesus took away 3 of them, representing 25%. Part of your problem is the 25% timeframes of your life. You and I were affected by the 25% time away from our leader's syndrome. Things go missing from your life 25% of the time. Time is costly, and we're forced to spend much of it. In other words, God allowed me to see it this way because he said it represented the 25% increments of my mom being away from me in the real world. And while she was away, he said, where was the other 75% of your time spent?..... Jesus and the inner circle came down the mountain and met with the other 75% of life, the outer circle, and the rest of the world. My mom was bringing me down, and I was left in the care of the outer circle and the rest of the world. Yeah, I started to see this as the beginning of problems. I started looking at it this way; 25% of my time was spent sleeping, 25% in school, 25% in the care of outer circle kin folks, and 25% leftover with Mom. The valley is like a vast hole that everyone falls into. The valley is where 75% of our time is spent. The valley is where I was forced to defend myself against cruelty in schools or outside the neighborhood. It's where I had to stand alone and feel like an outsider inside the outer circle of kindred folks. We often hear that most molestations happen inside the outer circle, so forget the *"cruelty of the world"* cliche; most cruelty comes from circles of families in the valleys......

So how protected, did you feel without the presence of your leader or your *"inner circle"*? The disciples were facing a healing and deliverance crisis without the presence of Jesus. Can you imagine being in that situation? If you believe in Christ, can you heal and deliver without Jesus' physical presence? Think about what I'm saying. I'm sure there was some fear around this situation because of the intimidation of the crowd, the religious scholars, and this dumb spirit acting up in front of everyone. It burned bricks everywhere, and they were lost in who they were. And being bold and confident comes easy when you have someone with authority standing behind you. But who will stand for you when they're gone 50% of the time? Do you feel like this dumb spirit thats afraid to speak up for yourself amid other family members and the rest of the world? Were you afraid to ask for something because you didn't want to feel like a burden or in the way of others? Were you afraid of any backlash or comments you overheard about you and your inner circle struggles? If you're a parent with children and you entrust them in the care of your other family members 50% of the time, start to pay attention to their faces and presence around you. Trust me when I say this, your child is picking up other spirits from the outer world and your outer circle most of the time. As I explained, their responses tell you what's going on. Imagine you, as a parent picking up your child late at night, and he's begging you for food. You need clarification about why he didn't eat but check his facial expression responses. You wonder why your child used to be one way, but now they end up another way; well, where were they 75% of the time? If you are the child and notice a shift, where are you 75% of the time? The scripture says this boy possessed a dumb spirit and could not speak. For most of my life, people thought of me as shy. Shyness comes from an oppressing spirit that causes you to fear what other people think about you, and it enables you from speaking. Mom/Dad, your lil boy/girl is growing up and spending 50% of the time with other spirits. The parent of this boy told Jesus he had been like this since childhood. Since childhood, you grew up secretly upset and in silence because you couldn't speak up for yourself. You were afraid to express what you experienced, and this dumb spirit robbed you and left you in an emotional pit. You know your parents loved you, but your face doesn't show it. Your responses to life show that something is missing, and it's hard for you to get with the picture now.

As I strolled through that photo album with God, I knew something was wrong with my picture that I didn't want to face. It's the same problem you have, the same problem your parents probably had; it's the same problem these disciples had. I titled this chapter Know Love and Power because it represents all of us; me, you, and these disciples. The disciples knew the power, but they had no power. In other words, they knew the one with power, but that power didn't get to them, and their faces showed it. Their response to this life crisis showed that something was missing that didn't get in them. My expression in life showed that I was missing love.

I knew my mom's love for me, but only 25% got inside. It's no different with you. You have knowledge of love that was around you, but only 25% got inside. The disciples had little knowledge of Jesus around them, but only 25% of them got to see the inside. I've known love but didn't have love. You've known love but don't have love. The disciples knew power but didn't have power. Love was around me but didn't get in me. Love was around you but didn't get in you. The disciples had power around them, but the power didn't get to them.

Do you hear and see us in this equation? No love and no power/Know love and Know power?....

So as you can see, time is expensive, and I'm sure you're grasping this revelation now. This little boy had crowds pointing fingers and talking about him. The same may be true about you now. You look and feel like an outsider, and you're behavior is abnormal to the rest of the world. You feel and see yourself differently and are ashamed of how your parents look at you. You've probably already heard these words before, *"what in the world happened to you, or what in the world got into you?"* With this chapter, it's not really what got into you that I wanted you to see. It's what didn't get into you. You see, you have a love deficit for receiving and giving genuine love. In other words, you lack felt love, and that anger and depressed facial expression shows the loneliness and sense of belonging inside. That mask of inner loneliness covers the lack of affection you yearn for, and it seems hopeless because you don't see a way of escape. But here's some hope for you, you've already spent 25% of your time with me in this book, and 75% of it is left. And as your Spiritual brother now, you are a part of my inner circle, and I want that image of me to grasp your awareness. 75% of what you needed didn't get in you, but I will show you precisely what you did and still can.

CHAPTER FOUR
My Shot Was Taken

It's 11:37 p.m., and the sound of aggressive voices awakens me. I got up and slowly twisted the handle to crack my door slightly. *"I wish your son would run in here now,"* I overheard, followed by gurgling words of *"Stop it, let me go"*! My heart dropped, and I knew what the commotion was about, so I took a few steps back. I opened my closet to feel for clothes and quietly got dressed.

My legs were shaken as I kept glancing for any approaching shadows towards my door. As I tightened my drawstring, I immediately reached for the 45-magnum pistol I had tucked away in the corner.

I kept rehearsing the thoughts of promises I made to myself. *"I swear to God, the next time this happens, I swear I'm going to do something about it!"*. The commotions continued as I heard the tussle and furniture movements across the floor. The cursing and stampede grew louder, ending with a hard door slam. At this point, it's complete silence, and my eyes are glued to the small crack of light. 10 seconds later, I heard footsteps walking and the blood pump in my chest. As it sped up, I nervously raised my aim in front of me as the steps finally approached. It swung open, the lights quickly switched on, and my shot was taken............... As the police wrapped up the scene, I walked before my mom and said, *"I have something to tell you."* I told her I was locked, loaded, and prepared for war. Her eyes widened as she became aware of what I was saying. She dropped her head while her shakey hands covered her eyes and said, *"Oh lord Sherwin, what has gotten into you!"* I stood there speechless and in confusion, thinking I became a man because of what I carried. She was disturbed and realized that the man was becoming a part of me because of what he carried. We both had possessions taking complete control, which sounded off her alarm. She always intended to protect me from the outside world, but now an outside war has become an inside battle.

Consider this story round 1 of the battle. It's like me sitting at this bar waiting for the bartender to pour me another round. I reminisce on life like this empty shot glass waiting to be filled. Right now, it sits on this table with a void, and it has me thinking the same about you and the empty world of people. We crave to be filled with something that depresses empty feeling inside. Shot glasses, bottles, humans, it's all the same analogy. We're all made to be poured in or poured out in that image. I started to be filled when my mom introduced me to a man who became my stepfather. He stepped up to the void I was missing and began giving me a taste of manhood. Now listen, if you could read my words, know I didn't like you first. I was a mama's boy growing up with me filling up her time besides work. But hear you come, tagging along with us, taking up my space. I thought you were going to be like any other guy that didn't take my mom seriously, but for some reason, you stuck around. You became another voice in the house that I had to learn to respect. I already had an Image that I knew of love, but this new Image of you was foreign to me. The label you presented read: 100% man (41 proof). At 41, you stepped into a role in my life as a father figure. You lived half your life and traveled down this manhood road. You didn't have to do it, but I'm glad you have been honest. You said you were done working hard and raising kids, but I guess I started a new beginning for you. You saw something in me that I couldn't see in myself. You taught me things about you through some phrases you spoke. I love to remember one of your phrases: *"It's another day in the jungle."* I didn't know what you meant by that, but life clarified the definition as I got older. The jungle is the way life looks through your eyes. The jungle consists of crabs by the seashore waiting to be caught in buckets of comparisons. How hard it was as a man to get up in systems of the land to eat and survive. How the two shades on the front and back side of my hands showed a difference in who I chose to work for in life.

The jungle consisted of some conniving and sneaky women, and how I needed to cover my head and learn to protect my heart. I can remember us walking by the sea, and you opened my eyes to varieties of fish. I laugh inside because I recall a few of them I brought back to you and you insisted that I toss them back in the ocean. In the jungle, you opened my eyes to the pawn shops filled with easily accessed weapons. I'll never forget when you requested me to need target practice because I was always shooting with my eyes closed. And not to mention the gun laws, but you taught me the street laws as well. Rules like never flash it in an altercation if I don't use it. Or think hard before I shoot. Yeah, these were a few good lessons I learned in daylight hours, but the jungle gets dark at night. It's so dark sometimes that seeing what's right in front of you is hard.

The jungle can camouflage infestations of the walking dead with addictions. It has locations where human body activities become strange for a little change. The jungle also consists of package shops, which light up the most at night. I used to watch you walk in and come out with that black bag. And I became curious to see what was so special about people flooding the insides, so I followed you. Upon opening the door, I first noticed a royal chair with purple fabric around it and a crown nestled in the middle. I'll never forget it. They advertised that Canadian whiskey well. They had cases stacked neatly all around them, and their royal Image got my attention. It seemed impossible to have a party in the jungle without a little alcohol.

Well, at least that's what I thought. Because I could walk inside to see the difference in liquors, I made my picks by how attractive the bottles were labeled on the outside. But I didn't realize how strong and bitter it was on the inside. The taste was awful, and the tolerance was foreign to me. I was being fooled by the Image of the bottle that also came with warnings and fine prints. The warnings were there to remind me of the responsibilities that come with it, and I saw why. It's like walking into the store, and the owner says, *"You're free to pick your poison."* Now, the battle of this poison affects you in three stages, and I had to learn that as well. The first is how the Image is packaged and presented to your eyes. The second is the taste inside and how it makes you feel in the moment. The third is the aftermath of how it makes you feel the next day. I never forgot my choice of crown royal, just like I never forgot you. The Image of you is like the Image of their brand. At first, I wouldn't say I liked the taste of it, but over time, my tolerance increased. Their brand is like a representation of your Image. What you presented on the outside, what was inside you, and how you made me feel afterward. This Image of the crown was to represent a king of a family. And you became the king of our royal family. In the family, the king is the head of the household, the support system underneath the home, the structure of the walls around, and a covering above. But watching you made me realize that some kings have holes in their walls, leaks in their roofs, and weaknesses underneath.

Another day in the jungle was like watching another episode of Naked and Afraid. A man and woman come together to survive in jungles, islands, rainforests, and deserts with only raw materials. They had to build themselves shelters, hunt for food and water, and survive to the finish with the risk of becoming ill, giving up, and facing death. Every season showed new jungles and came with new challenges. The same is true with you and I. Im sharing my episodes with you in this book, but you also came from a jungle of your own. And know that the islands as we see it may appear as a paradise to the world in daylight but try surviving on it alone with nothing at night. Now this show starts with a meet and greet of a naked man and woman. I can imagine the awkwardness of standing in front of a stranger naked, but in front of the world is different. Just think about the cameras and the world watching you struggling in nakedness to survive. That's the real fear of it all, and I'm ready to teach you something about this. So here's the crazy thing, we all live naked and afraid. We all live in life episodes, and it's no different from the Bible.

The first episode of Naked and Afraid was with Adam and Eve in the beginning. God created Adam and made Eve his helpmate. They both had a meet n greet. They both were in a jungle around wild animals; they had to learn to survive, they only had raw materials, and they had the world watching. This was the first royal family and the representation of the Image of God. The two joined naked and weren't afraid, but the world watched them. They represented a family surviving in a jungle and showed how the world came in. When my mom asked what got into me, it was no different from how the world got into the first royal family. The world is like a jungle with light and darkness—the two sides of a story or two meanings of an episode. God desired a man and a woman to join together and build a home. But like you and me, most homes have fathers that are absent or fathers with voids and holes. Adam was built strong in the lord, but his weakness was his woman, the wound from his flesh. Now I want you to catch this in 3 Dimensions.

God put Adam to sleep and surgically removed Eve from his side. When she joined him, *"Adam said, this is now bone of my bone and flesh of my flesh."* Adam had a hole in his side that he eventually healed from. His wife, Eve, was the missing piece of him that made him whole with a *"W."* But she represents that hole in his flesh, and the hole is always a portal for entry. My point is that women are a weakness for many men, so before you get offended, read about it throughout the Bible. Most kings fell from grace because of a woman. As I said, it is no difference in our stories. The world came in through a woman, which was Eve. The world represents satan that deceived Eve with seeds of suggestions to get Adam to sin. And he was always there watching from the beginning of the episode. He sees the weaknesses, the voids, and holes of homes trying to be built, and that's where he comes in. Eve is the Image of every woman, and satan is watching and always taking notes.

So what got into me came through my mom first. It's like a pattern satan uses, and the war is always about destroying homes by getting to the man and seeds. He uses women to do both. Please look at our world and think about what I'm saying. All the episodes of what life was supposed to look like are now twisted by satan. His demolition work is seen throughout the world. To get at God, I'll use the man. To get to the man, I'll use woman. I'll use seeds (children, suggestions) to get to a woman. Look at the pornographic industries, strip clubs, films, and music videos. All of it is for men to fantasize and lust over a woman. Women can care about all that. How many male strip clubs can you count? Or how about our young boys and men who are twisted about their image of being a woman? A lot of boys appear as girls and vice versa. The war poured into the houses, the bottles, and the humans, and that spirit twisted the caps and had everyone filled. The royal family was built on God's foundations, protections, and connections, but when the world of sin came in, the connection broke. See it as the power cut off and the internal Net being disconnected. Without the connection of our Heavenly Father in our houses, it created the beginning of voids. And when you've grown in roots of voids, you tend to seek *"feel-ings"* on the outside to bring in on the inside. Some outside fill-ins are established right down your street. Package shops are an easy suggestion and not hard to find. And when you hear the word package in shops, please think of the invisible warnings packed on the inside. Resembling Eve being tempted in the garden.

The Garden of Eden had warnings that came with the package of the forbidden fruits. *"God said, if you partake of it, you will certainly die"* (Genesis 2:17). In this 3D episode, I want to show you its three lessons, three temptations, and three stages. The first is the lesson of death. Death is a separation of life and the consequences of committing sins against God, and we experience three. Physical, spiritual, and eternal. Because they sinned against God, they immediately experienced spiritual death, the loss of spiritual connections from the disruption of sin. That connection can be reestablished by repenting and accepting Jesus Christ as your Lord and Savior. I needed to throw that in there so you can experience spiritual life again, but let's continue. Eternal death is separation from God forever in the lake of fire. And physical death, as we all know, is the separation from our physical bodies, which begins a slow process of body decay. Death as a whole is the absents of abundant life with God. Physically, spiritually and eternally. The second lesson is the three temptations. Genesis 3:6- "When the woman saw that the fruit of the tree was good for food and pleasing to the eye, and also desirable for gaining wisdom, she took some and ate it. She also gave some to her husband, who was with her, and he ate it. The biggest weapon satan uses is suggestions. Suggestions are his way of getting you twisted to focus on what you want, what will make you feel good, and how great you would appear to others in the now. In other words, that's his power of temptation and the ability he uses to influence your thoughts, feelings, and behavior. This psychological phenomenon impacts your behavior, beliefs, and attitudes that influence how you perceive yourself and others around you. He impacts how you make decisions and how you respond in different situations. No wonder God put warnings in the garden because it was intoxication inside. Intoxication has a significant impact on your thoughts and behavior, and it has the power to make you drop the guards of your image. Just pay attention to someone who is intoxicated. You will notice how relaxed and open they become, even around strangers. The automatic filters they've set on their image will be in default. If they're normally shy at a party, this liquid courage has them feeling too good at the moment to focus on how others perceive them. Or better yet, this liquid courage will make a person's heart speak loudly when upset. If you want to hear what's inside a person's heart, wait until they're pissed off and intoxicated, and you will pick up on some truths.

Now I twisted all of this together so you can notice this episode in the garden and what has happened in our lives. Package shops are always planted nearby, just like this forbidden fruit tree was planted nearby, and they both come with temptation. The three temptations that are always used by satan are the lust of the eye, the lust of the flesh, and the pride of life. The lust of the eye refers to an intense desire for something material or worldly pleasure that's visually appealing, which can lead to wrongdoings. Or when a person has a visual perception or attraction to beauty. The lust of the flesh refers to an intense desire or craving for physical pleasure and gratification. This can include things like overindulging in food, or alcohol, engaging in sexual activity without regard for moral and ethical considerations, or engaging in other behaviors that provide immediate physical pleasure but can have negative consequences in the long term. The pride of life refers to an excessive focus on one's achievements, possessions, or status. This term can be used more generally to describe excessive focus on material success or social status and a tendency to prioritize these things over other values, such as kindness and spiritual well-being. This could include constantly seeking recognition or approval from others, competing for status or recognition, or being overly attached to material possessions as a source of identity or self-worth. Now I can stop here and suggest that you make a checklist with your heart and see if satan intoxicated you. You will recognize him when suggestions come within these three temptations. And if he's constantly making these suggestions in your ears, I want you to tell him I suggest you go to hell. And you can tell him big brother said it too. But suggestions are always packaged through weaknesses, voids, holes, and in this episode, Eve/women! All of it starts with the eye, and the rest follows in order, so remember that.

I followed in the footsteps of my void, which was my stepfather, and started to lust over that royal bottle. It was unforbidden for me to touch, but the beauty was attractive to my eyes, and I constantly thought of how it would feel. So I picked my poison, twisted off the top, and realized the power inside. The taste started the death process of my last lesson on the three stages. The taste of death is the same as the taste of sin, and Adam and Eve became aware of the effects in three areas. Genesis 3:7-8 reads, *"And the eyes of them both were opened, and they knew that they were naked, and they sewed fig leaves together, and made themselves aprons. And they heard the voice of the Lord God walking in the garden in the cool of the day, and Adam and his wife hid from the presence of the Lord god amongst the garden's trees."*

The first stage of effect is self-awareness. Self-awareness refers to recognizing and understanding one's thoughts, emotions, and behaviors. In this case, they became aware of themselves as bottles that disregarded the warning label and were filled with guilt and shame. In other words, they realize they've just disobeyed the commands of God. The 2nd stage is the covering. The scripture says they used the fig leaves to make themselves aprons. Aprons are garments worn over clothing to protect it from dirt, stains, and any other forms of damage while doing work. Well, they were naked and had a job to do in the garden, but the damage was already done. They immediately *"felt"* the guilt and shame and tried to use something from the outside to cover and protect what was on the *"inside."* It was an immediate response that took control over them. Just think about something you think is wrong, and you did it anyway; your immediate response will be to try and cover it up yourself. Test the words that I'm speaking and think about walking outside naked. The immediate response of your flesh instantly wants to grab something and cover-up.

Now the last stage is running. I call it the running stage because they tried to blend in with the surrounding trees. God was looking for them, and they ran and hid. Look at it as a parent searching for their child. Your parents know who you were when you came into the world, but as you've gotten older, you started running with another crowd. You had a taste of the high, and you immediately wanted to blend in with the rest. Now, on the run, you're ashamed of the fig leaves you're addicted to. Adam and Eve were aware of themselves, but the minute they had a taste, they no longer liked themselves. This unforbidden fruit had power, and the leaves were the controlled substance. The bite activated the death process that progressed slowly. I'm teaching this way because slow death increases as your craving for sin increases. Here's a good example most adults can relate to, especially men. Sex before marriage is like unforbidden fruit in the jungle of life. And the minute you bite it, you will surely die. I know most people won't talk about this topic or feel uncomfortable talking about it, but God created sex in the marriage for procreation and also for pleasure. But for some strange reason, these unforbidden trees were planted everywhere. And the fruits were all in the marketplaces, and some reached our homes. I know this well because I found some of the fruits under my stepfather's mattress. Yep, I found the peachy magazines and the packaged VHS tapes, and what I constantly watched made me aware of my nature, and that started to crave a taste. My eyes became addicted first, but my desire for how I wanted to feel was next. On the outside, it was easy to pick the fruits that matched the beauty of what I was seeing on the inside. So when the poison was finally picked, and I began to taste, my eyes were open, and it started the slow death process. Every man can attest to what I'm saying, once you get that first taste of sin, the craving increases. The addiction takes control and have you leaving the house to seek more fruits. The slow death occurs because God never designed it that way. Your tolerance for more forces you to overindulge, and now it has the power to control you.

Marriage life was supposed to be a sober intimate place of pleasure, but we tend to show up with high tolerance and intoxication. Overindulging with alcohol is no different. Taste is influential, and it has the power to take over and control life. Well, maybe I was twisted and missed some warning labels, but I thought all this in the jungle was just the taste of a man's life.

So what was getting into me was a natural flavor of manhood, but this came through the relationship between my mom and you. Your presence poured into the house, and some other things spilled into me as well. I started to focus on my status as a man and paid attention to my strengths. Knowing better now, I noticed how the spirits in that bottle took over you. They call it spirits for a reason. It's distilled beverages made by distilling fermented grains, fruits, or veggies. The *"spirits"* comes from the alchemical tradition of distillation, initially thought to be extracting a substance's spirit or essence. The distillation process separates the alcohol from the other components of the fermented mixture, resulting in a stronger, more concentrated alcoholic beverage. And I watched all of this strength being poured into you. You allowed these spirits to fill you, and that image became larger. I felt as if I was intimidated by a large shadow that followed me around on walls. Confusion and fear started to fill me because I thought you understood the labels and fine print. I could not understand what influenced your behavior to become this angry and aggressive. So I finally swallowed some courage to do something about it.

That night, two spirits met in the middle of the house—one spirit in anger and the other in fear. And what stood in between that war was my door. It was a matter of time before this moment presented itself again, so I ensured I was equipped. As the front door slammed, I knew this was my chance; I knew this was my opportunity, or in my terms, I knew this was my *shot*! I was determined to end all this, and the door swung open. Before the light switched on, there was an immediate flash in my eyes. My shot was taken! I wanted to end all of this, so I aimed at that controlling spirit inside you. But the thought of pulling that trigger flashed before my eyes, and all I could see was a broken glass bottle. The 10 seconds it took for your footsteps to approach my door was enough time for me to make this permanent decision. My target was the spirit, but the aim was pointed at you. I really had my shot, but the love for you took it away. So I rushed under the covers, laid on the gun, and closed my eyes.

When you switched the lights, I held my breath and pretended to be asleep. The words you poured into me were racing all around my mind. At that moment, I heard you clearly saying to me, never shoot with your eyes closed! Only flash it if I'm going to use it! Think before you shoot in any altercations! So finally, when my door shut, I exhaled and opened my eyes. The next thing I knew was flashing blue lights outside. My mom rushed out of the house to call law enforcement to come and escort you away. And as they wrapped up the scene, I approached her with the secret behind my door, and that was the last night you physically removed from our house.

My momma dared to remove the world from me like a bartender removing my shot glass. But my mind became twisted now, and I needed to sober. Your fight became my fight, and I'm writing in 2nd person because I wish you were here to read what I have to say. I wanted you to know when I saw you; I saw a void. You were my royal crown bottle but filled with another spirit. I had a shot at destroying that spirit, but it was taken. You battled that spirit for a long time, and it finally got the best of you. It took you away, and I couldn't make it to speak up for you at your funeral. So I decided to share this story and your words with the world. I wanted you to know that everything you poured into me wasn't bitter. A lot of it was sweet. Your favorite was another day in the jungle, but you showed me more. You used to tell me all the time to *"watch your ass out there."* I knew the jungle was hard to grow up in, and you didn't want me to get caught up with the wrong crowds. My favorite lesson was when you said, *"Ima show you what you don't want to do."* Well, at the time, I enjoyed going to work with you, but after a while, the reality of it hit hard. I was working at a young age, and making more money than the average sounds good to my ears.

All I could think about was buying the shoes and clothes I wished you could afford when I complained. I learned to respect getting up at 4 a.m. every morning with you and working for a man who watches over us all day. I know you wanted me to taste what the workforce world only had to offer by doing jobs I didn't like, so I followed you. I wish I had listened earlier and done better with schooling. But my chosen career path worked out in my favor because of you. You taught me how to drive well since 15, and my passion grew for driving. Because of that, I'm glad I could show you the back country roads cross country in my semi truck.

It's bittersweet writing this because you knew your life was ending, but it was one thing you couldn't be honest about. It feels like the last conversation we had on your rooming house couch, and you screamed, *"How in the hell did I get here"*? And I felt some pain as you spoke that aloud. You reached into the drawer and pulled out an old high school prom picture of you and your girlfriend. I had never seen you that happy before and looked that good simultaneously. I was amazed that you kept this photo for over 30 years. But as you reminisced and opened your heart more, my eyes opened. You've been holding on to some pain inside for a long time, and alcohol was just a bandage.

After all these years, you were bleeding a life you didn't choose and needed healing. No wonder you told me I'd never become wealthy by working for someone else. You worked all your life to try and be the image of a man, only to come to the end of it with nothing to show. You died in the jungle you didn't want me in. But I'm a firm believer in actions than words. The taste you left in my mouth is bitter because you gave up the fight. Your life was coming to an end, and mine was beginning. I have my own sons now, and I wanted us to show them how to blaze another path. You showed me what I didn't want, but I was trying to show you what you did want. You were proud of me when I started driving trucks because your dad wanted you to do that with your life. I told you it wasn't too late and I would be the one to teach you. I thought the bottle was in the way, but I realized it was something empty in you.

When I started ministering, I wanted you to learn that the tongue is the fastest healing part of your natural body, and God said the power of life and death is in the tongue. Spiritually speaking, (*"Ezekiel 47:12 talks about fruit trees growing on both river banks. Their leaves will not wither, nor will their fruit fail. Every month they will bear fruit because the water from the sanctuary flows to them. Their fruit will serve for food and their leaves for healing."*) **You see, God** was available to us all along and was there in the jungle. All we had to do was look for his fruit trees and water on the other side of the jungle, and we could've been filled and healed. But I know the tolerance was too great, and you left me searching for it alone. You were the shot glass that was taken away from me. When you died, a part of me died with you. But the twist for me is figuring out which part of me went with you. I prayed my image of Christ made an impact on your life just like your image made an impact on mine. When I get to the other side, I hope to find a royal crown on your head, but until then, I will spread this word and continue my days in this jungle.

Until I see you again;

Love,

Your son.

CHAPTER FIVE
The Weapon Formed Against You

I opened my front door, looked around, and up towards the sky. Grey clouds were forming, and the trees seemed like they were waving goodbye to me. Time was ticking, and I needed to make a decision. Our bags were packed, but I had two directions in mind. I quickly grabbed the phone and made a call. When the receptionist picked up, I asked if the event was still happening on Sunday. She said as of now, the path of the storm just missed us, and everything is still on schedule. I hung up and took a deep breath. My decision is made, and we're heading south, I said. I'm sure my wife saw a nervous facial expression, and I don't think she expected me to say that, but I couldn't let this opportunity pass me. We were right in the middle of hurricane season off the coast of

Ga, but I was right in the middle of a season of faith. At least, I thought. My location was Savannah, GA, but my destination was Miami, FL. It was a straight shot to get there on I-95 South, but Matthew was in my way. Now I want you to understand my thought process during this time. You may find some humor within this chapter. My dream growing up was to play in the NBA. Of course, that was a dream growing up; that was the majority of all our childhood dreams, but we know in the real world, that seems impossible for the average.

In the world of Christianity, all things are possible to him that believes, right? In this season of my life, I was getting deeper in my spiritual walk and came across these signs along my path. Motivational voices were everywhere, making me pay attention to the *"don't give up on your dreams"* sayings. I held on to this dream for a while, and my only chance of opportunity was to try out for the NBA development league finally—a minor league under the NBA. Basketball is like playing on different levels of a video game. Every level gets harder as you go up, and these levels are like doors to pass through. I missed going through the high school's front door and the college's next door, so I saw a back door of entry to my dream. I started researching a few guys that took this route and got inspired by what I found. I was looking for people closest to my age range, so

I started my little training. And despite having to work my job, being involved in church, and my wife just conceiving, I prepared for tryout season anyway for the fall. I already paid my entry fee months ahead, and my time finally came in October. But as I said, hurricane Matthew was on its way toward us. Now this is where it got tricky in my mind. The behavior of hurricanes usually makes curves in their paths, but this year, it decided to straighten up just for me. Yeah, I took it personally because it made landfall just above Miami and decided to ride the coast of FL up I-95 straight toward us. If you research it for yourself, you will see what I mean. Now I'm thinking this can't be a coincidence.

Suddenly, I prepare to try the impossible in my life, but a storm breaks out in my path to deter my faith. Yeah, right, I'm going for it in my thoughts. At this time, I'm 33 years old, there is no refund, and I'm not getting any younger. All year I heard the word being preached about *"your faith will be tested "*and *"your faith will be tested,"* my mind was blown away, thinking that it would be an actual storm in my way. I felt this chapter of my life was like what the disciples experienced at the end of chapter 4 in the gospel of Mark. This identical life reads like this: (*"Late that day, he said to them, let's go across to the other side. They took him in the boat as he was, and a huge storm came up. Waves poured into the boat, threatening to sink it. And Jesus was in* *the stern, head on a pillow, sleeping! They roused him, saying, Teacher, is it nothing to you that we're going down? Awake now, he told the wind to pipe down and said to the sea, Quiet! Settle down! The wind ran out of breath; the sea became smooth as glass. Jesus reprimanded the disciples: Why are you acting cowardly? Don't you have any faith?" - Mark 4:35-40).* **You see, I thought I was reliving a chapter in the Bible because my destination was on the other side of the storm. My city was evacuating north, but my faith wanted to head south. After all this research and training, I was determined to see what was on the other side. I was confident that God was with me and that this chapter of my life was about to be over.**

As you turn the page from the ending my chapter 4 to the beginning of chapter 5, you see I titled it *"The weapon formed against you."* At the beginning of Mark chapter 5, Jesus reached the destination intended. It's the other side of the story I believe the disciples had rather not face, and it replicates another side of my story I didn't want to face. It's another side of your story that you may not want to turn and face, but that's where the weapons form against you. Meaning after the storm, you face the truth of the devil. I know the saying, *"new level/new devil,"* but I'll first say there's nothing new about him. He's the same as he has always been since his job termination in Heaven. And he was able to influence a third of Heaven's angels to follow him down here in different regions on Earth. Now Jesus and the disciples made landfall and immediately met with these devils. The passage reads: *("They made across the lake to the region of Gerasenes. When Jesus exited the boat, a man with an unclean spirit(demon) came from the tombs to meet him. The man lived in the tombs, and no one could bind him anymore, not even with chains. He has often been chained hand and foot, but he tore the chains apart and broke the irons on his feet. No one was strong enough to subdue him. Night and day among the tombs and hills, he would cry out and cut himself with stones. When he saw Jesus from a distance, he ran and fell to his knees in front of him. He shouted at the top of his voice, "What do you want with me, Jesus, Son of the Most High God? Have you come to torture me before the time? Jesus said to him, "Come out of this man, you unclean spirit! Then Jesus asked him, What is your name? My name is Legion, he replied, for we are many. And he repeatedly begged Jesus not to send them out of the territory. A large herd of pigs was feeding on the nearby hillside. The demons begged Jesus to send us among the pigs; allow us to go into them. He permitted them, and the unclean spirits came out and entered the pigs. The herd, about 2000, rushed down the steep bank into the lake and were drowned - Mark 5:1-13).* **Now it's a lot I want to discuss with this, and the 1st thing is the response of Legion as his name. In the Bible, the Legion is referred to as a large group of Roman soldiers. Considerably several thousands of soldiers. But it's the name of a particular demon I want to bring some attention to.**

This event represents a kind of spiritual warfare and has something to do with your name. Especially your last name.

In spiritual warfare, names represent individuals' or spiritual entities' identity and nature. Knowing the names can help identify their power, purpose, and intent and enable you to address them appropriately with authority and respect. Look at this passage closely. Do you see the respect of the demon approaching Jesus? *"I know who you are, Jesus, the son of God, said the spirit."* The name Jesus invokes a powerful weapon against evil spirits, and they knew it. This is a battle of names in spiritual combat. The spirit acknowledged Jesus by name, and they responded with their name. Now I'm bringing this to your attention because it's a war going on, and your name came up in it. It's a war with weapons that will be used against you. People will prejudge you based on the name you have. For instance, the fruits don't fall far from the tree sayings. The results of your behavior can be tracked by how your parents presented themselves in the world. Or what about *"he acts just like his daddy"* or *"she gets it from her momma"*? These are examples of mindsets and habits based on the name behind you, and this is where weapons form. In other words, this is where generational curses come into play. A generational curse traditionally associates with negative afflictions passed down from one generation to the next due to sins and actions from previous ancestors.

One concept of these curses is often based on the teaching that God will visit the iniquities of the fathers upon the children to the third and fourth generation - Exodus 20:5. Commentators interpret this to mean that the consequences of sin can be passed down to future generations, leading to negative patterns of behavior, health issues, financial struggles, or other afflictions. I didn't care about all those sayings, but my life started revealing some truths behind this. As I grew as a man, I noticed that my life resembled my biological dad's. My biggest red flag was that I have two kids a year apart by two different women. And my half-sister and I are a year apart by two different women. The problem with this scenario is I was born 1st in marriage, but my sister was born a year later out of marriage. In my life, My 1st son was conceived by another woman out of marriage, but the next year my wife and I conceived our son in marriage. Wait a minute! I followed a pattern that I didn't see. Two women, two kids, a year apart, one in marriage, one out of marriage, and this transpired in the same timeframe? Of course, I wasn't paying attention to all this then, but I noticed the resemblance later. My life was starting to reflect in the mirror of an invisible man. He wasn't around in my life for me to learn this from him, so something else must be going on. Becoming someone you didn't see can be discerned in a good and bad way. In a good way, you pick up some matching gifts and talents. You may grow with some of the same interests and desires. But in a bad way, you pick up negative behavior patterns or similar health issues. You may wonder why you struggle to get past a financial level or a health crisis. Well, it's because your parents never got passed it. In the spirit world, it's both good and bad spirits, and the bad ones can be assigned to your last name. This is the other side of your identity and represents the internal region we will explore.

I want you to picture your image as a sea divided by your first and last name. One side of you is the region where your identity is based on your first name. Your identity based on your last name is on the other side of your region. Now the disciples had a calling to follow Jesus, and you have a calling to follow Jesus. Throughout the Bible, God continually called man by his first name, not his whole name. He does that to show you a separation in your identity from who you are and where you came from. As we can see, Jesus called these disciples in a boat to cross from one side of the region to the other side. The other side of the sea is the unclean side of you and symbolically is where the pigs are. Let me explain more. Jesus deliberately crossed the Sea of Galilee, which was predominantly

Jewish territory, to reach the gentile region of the Gerasenes. This showed that Jesus' ministry was not limited to the Jewish people but extended to the Gentiles. It's showing you his message and mission to bring salvation and deliverance to you regardless of your background or where your name came from. The pigs' presence in this story shows how they were considered unclean animals to the Jewish dietary laws, and their presence in this Gentile region suggests a departure from Jewish religious customs and norms. By allowing the unclean spirits to enter the pigs, Jesus shows you his authority over the spiritual realm and the power to liberate any demonic possession. The demons begged Jesus not to leave the territory, and this shows you how and where the weapons are being formed against you.

Before heading to the other side, I lived consciously within my first region most of my life. But I got the call from God, and that 3D story began something like this:

God said, "SHERWIN"!

I turned around and said, "Yes! Who's there"?

God said, "It's ME! Now listen up..... You're about to go into war".

I said, "A war with who"?

He said, "Satan"!

I responded, "Oh..........Ok".

Starring at me, he said, "You're about to face him head-on"!

I said, "What do you mean"?

He responded, "Follow me to the other side, and I'll show you"!

So as we started sailing in the realm of the spirit, nothing was unusual at first, and I became less interested. My thoughts were trying to comprehend what God was trying to teach, but I began to doze off. Suddenly the boat rocked as the winds and the waves started to pick up, and I instantly woke up to see what was happening. As I looked around, I began to see things in the middle of my heart that I didn't know existed. This was a spiritual storm with gusty winds of words and intense waves of emotions that came against me. I looked around for God, and I couldn't see him. But his voice yelled from below, saying, *"Draw nigh to God, and he will draw nigh to you. Cleanse your hands ye sinners; and purify your hearts, ye double-minded"*-James 4:8. And again, *"whenever our hearts convicts us (in guilt); for God is greater than our heart and he knows all things (nothing is hidden from Him because we are in His hands)"*-1 John 3:20. Feelings of guilt started to rise in my heart about past sins I committed. And knowing that the captain of the ship was also the Eternal Judge made it difficult for me to stop my life-threatening thoughts. But I could hold a sturdy grip on his words as I struggled to stand while the storm passed. When it cleared, he walked up from the stern and approached me. I looked towards the *"ship's bridge"* and asked, *"Well, who was steering"*? And he skeptically said, *"It was on autopilot"*!

Now I wrote my story this way to show you that most of your storms in life are happening because of you. You, meaning your double mind of you having control of your life in one season and in other times you lose control. God is right there watching you live on autopilot and sees you being tossed around by every impulse that arouses you. Before you get to the other side of anything God says to you, a storm will always rise against you to show what's inside your heart. The storm reveals the division between where you're coming from and where you're headed. The guilt of what you did back there and anxiety of the unknown you're headed to now. I want you to remember that if you're heart convicts you, God already forgives you, and you can trust that in the middle of this type of storm.

Now the unknown becomes visible as you draw nigh to the other side. Fear of the unknown is a real feeling, especially when you have to face it. I've always heard about devils and demons, but it wasn't until we made landfall that he was revealed in the open field. I looked back on God's words and remembered him saying that I would face him head-on, and it's exactly what it sounds like. Facing his head-on is about a war in your mind. It would be best to remember demons are fallen, intelligent angels with power in darkness. Darkness is another word for ignorance; what you don't know can be used against you like a weapon. They are spiritual beings that cannot be seen with your natural eyes but can be discerned. Think about playing the game of hide n seek in your house. Before you seek their hiding, you should be able to sense their presence around the corner. But as you tiptoe around, one could be staring right at you without you recognizing him naturally. I'm saying it that way because they watched you all your life and saw you approaching the corners. Jesus is teaching that to you in scripture as he did with the disciples. He could see what we couldn't see. As Jesus landed, the demon immediately approached him, saying, *"Boy, you look just like you, Daddy." "I know exactly who you are, Jesus"*! And then he said, *"But wait, whatchu doing here"*? This was a scene of a Kingdom reunion. Meaning; Jesus already enlightened us about him, remembering how God kicked satan out of Heaven, and a third of them followed.

These same demons grew up around the Kingdom of Heaven and watched the bond of the Father and the Son. They know the power and authority he possesses from his Father. They know his inheritance and all the Kingdom real estate he owns. And a few of them eased dropped on the conversations God had when he thought about creating you. They knew you were fearfully and wonderfully made, so they intervened. They've studied all your habits and behaviors since you were a child. They know where you grew up and where you spent most of your time. I know this to be true because of Adam. God formed man from the dust of the ground. Everything about your flesh was shaped from the Earth. God placed the man called Adam in the garden but guess who was there already? The devil! He was watching when God formed your body, and he knows what foods you're supposed to eat and what not. We were supposed to rule the Earth as a whole family, but he intervened in that plan with his deceptive influence. He knows the background of our origin of humankind and your background. Your background is one territory demons like to hide, but I'm making them visible now. Demons know your Father like they know you. And they know you're Father's Father and so on. A few of them were assigned to the region you grew up in, and you can catch them playing around on the streets of your last name. They all have I-pads with your flesh DNA downloaded on the screen. And they've studied all your weaknesses and can make calculated suggestions about your thoughts.

The response to Jesus is the same response I've gotten, though. We made landfall, and I was approached head-on. He said,

"I know you just like your father." **The both of you look just alike. Yall have the same lifestyle! And I said,** *"Well, I resembled a long career in transportation just like you, and you abandoned me"! "I've learned things about myself that reflect your character!" "Because you disappeared and walked out that door, I had to search for another path alone"!* **I lost sight of who I was and needed to figure out what was ahead because of you! And because of that, momma was forced across the waters, and I had to navigate through that land to pick up other identities. This spirit looked at me and smirked. I picked up some learned behaviors independently but always felt the pull of something attached. I could never break free of these invisible strings and finally prayed for release. The answer I received was,** *"It's on the other side."*

I asked this demon, *"By the way, What is your name"? And he grinned, "Washington, for we are many!"* **For we are many represents a group of many members like a family reunion, just like your family reunions that gather in one place to connect and strengthen the family bonds. The gathering based on your last name can be seen as a village or a tribe. In other words, the** *"culture"* **of where you're from is one of the dark areas where you can find demonic activities. I couldn't see it on the opposite side of my life until I boarded the relationship with Jesus.**

As we walked away, Jesus pointed out to me four specific areas on this land. He said, *"These are the four areas where you can discern demonic activities in the world. They operate in these four areas to protect their power within systems. To the left is the area of principalities, to the right is the area of powers, where we just left is the area of the rulers of darkness, and further ahead is the area of spiritual wickedness. The principalities are the area governed by high-rank spirits over politics and governments. The area of power is economics. It's mainly driven under the authority of principalities in the business world. The area of spiritual wickedness deals with religion. These spirits are responsible for regions' religious, moral, philosophical, and spiritual identity. And we walked back to the last area, the rulers of darkness. This area deals with culture, he said. These spirits operate in entertainment through the media, arts, music, films, radio, formal and informal education, and sports. All these areas have one goal: to win influence in the dark. In the spirit realm, the competition is about good vs evil. But naturally, we must discern what is evil behind everything that appears good."*

I wondered how spirits fought in the spirit realm on the ship, and God must've heard my thoughts. I'm writing this chapter to show you some examples of these head-on encounters with spirits. That said, spirits fight with words of inspiration in your mind to influence your behavior. It's like human branding or stigmatizing. A word patterned to burn into your mind with the intention of making permanent scars. Jesus warned me on the ship to *"take up the shield of faith so I could block myself against the fiery arrows of words aimed at my head.-Ephesians 6:16"*. But I wasn't paying attention then and found myself detouring around a hurricane later.

So let me catch you up with that. That Friday evening, I studied the hurricane's speed to leave at a specific time. Because it made landfall and started up the coast, I planned to drive around the eye as I got closer towards in miles. We drove down to Jacksonville, FL, and I headed southwest towards Gainesville and stayed in a hotel until the storm passed Daytona and Jacksonville overnight. The anxiety passed as the storm passed, and I was clear to head south toward Miami. The first tryout session was at 8:30a.m. that Sunday, and I ate lightly to preserve my energy. I was surprised to find out what to expect besides the videos I researched on Youtube from other tryout participants. Now I managed to lose some truck driving weight, but I was about to learn that that wasn't enough. We had 15 minutes on the shot clock to shoot around and get loose. I looked around and noticed how serious everybody looked in the face and all the unnecessary stretches that were taking place. Now I'm thinking, why is everybody doing their pre-drills and burning all this energy before time? I was the only smart one in this group, so I paced around, sipping my water bottle. The buzzer went off, and the coaches gathered us at the baseline. He gave a welcome speech and introduced all the assistant coaches as they pep-talked to us. He explained everything that was about to happen in this tryout and wished us the best of luck. The first drill was full-court warm-ups. Let me tell you something, this was supposed to be a warm-up, but I called it a drill for a reason. As I mentioned, I lost a little trucking weight, but some of the fast food fat still lingered. I could've sworn I left it back in Savannah, but it decided to show up at *"the wrong time"*! The up-and-down warm-ups lasted for 15 minutes straight. And I was starting from the back of the line to catch my breath by the time I was up to the front again. After about the 3rd up and downs, I was the only one double-taking at the water fountains. My calves and thighs started to light up, and 25% of my inner fight was already depleted. We ended up splitting into four groups with 20-minute workout sessions apiece. The first session depleted me by 40 percent and the 2nd 30%. Two sessions left with 5% of my energy left, and I had to make a courageous decision. I looked around to see if any coaches were watching me, and for some strange reason, my planta pedis twisted. Thats right, I said it, my planta pedis!

Look it up for yourself since you're so bright! I ensured my limp game was on point as I headed towards the bench area to watch everybody else. When it was over, I thought we would wrap it up, and I could sneak out without looking like a coward. Names were being called to play in full-court games, and I was being called next." *Washington*"! It immediately grabbed my attention. The coach was calling players by their last names. I yelled back while pointing at my foot. He signaled me toward the Miami Heat injury personal trainers. I tried to explain what happened, but he tried his best to determine how this could be.

I laid there for the rest of the tryout with a poker face on the outside but cussing myself out on the inside. The ride home was one of the quietest but loudest rides ever. My mouth was shut, but my inner mind was arguing. It was saying things like what in the world made you do this. You almost passed out in the middle of the gym over some stupid dream you were pursuing. Who even convince you to do this in the first place? I rehearsed these thoughts over and over again. My pride was slapping me up and down the highway all the way home, but I managed to calm it down. When I finally reached the pillow, I reflected on the messages I followed to reach this point. I thought it was faith, but I started to 2nd guess it all. A lot of spiritual things transpired while I was on this journey. I remembered approaching a few intersections of contradicting words and a wilderness of confusion.

As I mentioned, I was following the motivational messages I was receiving, but then I bumped into a word that spoke like this, *"stop practicing; that is not your destination"*! Wait, what?.... Do I hear right? I paid it no mind and kept practicing and working out. Shoot, I'm walking by faith, devil, get out my way, in my mind! A month later, I remembered a message on the radio. Her exact words were, *"I blessed you with a wife, I blessed you with a house, but you are still failing the test"*! *"Can you see me?"*! Again, wait a minute! Why do I hear these kind of messages? Now I was walking in a mental state of confusion, but I continued until October.

After all of this passed, the journey started to get darker. The moon and stars were nowhere to light my path. The subliminal messages were hitting me from every angle without me noticing it. I tried to run, duck, and hide, but nothing worked. Negativity made its presence everywhere my eyesight turned, and I now started to have anxiety about my health, especially at night. It got so bad that I couldn't sleep without my left arm feeling like it was physically tightening up. I couldn't figure out why stress was at an all-time high. I couldn't say much because I thought I was tripping and felt like I was losing my mind. So I prayed in this darkness, and lights started showing up differently. In one direction, it showed up at a men's meeting I was attending. We studied the book *"The Battle of the*

Mind by Joyce Meyers," and one guy testified about his personal battle. He was experiencing similar situations, and it got so bad that he checked himself into a hospital to run tests. The doctors completed a full body exam and confirmed that nothing was wrong with him, so he knew it was all in his mind, but he couldn't figure out how. I kept quiet at the time, but I knew it was God showing me that I wasn't the only one fighting because I related to everything he said. Another answer came directly to me at night.

Again the anxiety was ridiculous, but a demon decided to make his presence known. Before I went to sleep that night, I was tuning in to a live bible study, and service was interrupted by a demon-possessed lady. She came to the front of the congregation, and the pastor cast it out. I noticed how bold this spirit was and how it fought her body as it was released. That image freaked me out, and I went to sleep with it on my mind. In the middle of my sleep, I saw that same lady's face, and it spoke to me saying *"heart attack"*! I jumped up, gasping for air, and rushed toward the back of the house, trying not to pass out. The power of words was striking me hard. I ran some cold water on my face to wake myself up fully with some deep breaths, and I was beginning to lose hope and fell into a hole of depression. I begged God to tell me why this was happening to me, and he decided to show me how it's been happening. He said, *"I'M*

In the Bible, there are two dangerous spirits I want you to become aware of. They are called lying and familiar spirits. They're dangerous because they are responsible for most of the spiritual warfare we see nowadays, especially in the religious and cultural areas. The lying spirit is the first one I want to break down. In 1 King 22:21-22, God gives you a glimpse inside the realm of spirits. It reads, *"Then a bold Angel stepped out, stood before God, and said, I'll seduce him. And how will you do it? God asked. It's easy, said the Angel, I'll be a lying spirit in the mouth of all his prophets"!* This story recounts a meeting between the kings of Israel and Judah, Ahab and Jehoshaphat, respectively, as they consider going to war against the city of Ramoth Gilead. They seek counsel from their prophets regarding the outcome of the battle. Ahab gathers about 400 prophets who all prophesy *"success"* and encourage him to go to war. However, Jehoshaphat requests to hear from a prophet who speaks for the Lord. Ahab reluctantly mentions Micaiah, a prophet who had previously been critical of him. When Micaiah is brought before the kings, he initially sarcastically agrees with the other prophets' positive prophecy.

However, upon Ahab's insistence, he reveals this vision where he sees the Lord seated on His throne and the angels surrounding Him. In Micaiah's vision, the Lord asks the angels who will entice Ahab to go to battle and fall. One spirit suggests becoming this lying spirit in the mouths of all the prophets, predicting Ahab's defeat and death in the battle at Ramoth Gilead. Upon hearing this, Ahab is displeased and imprisons Micaiah, commanding him to be kept on a limited diet until his return from the battle. Ahab disregards the warning and proceeds with the battle, disguised to avoid being targeted. However, a random arrow shot by an archer hits Ahab and mortally wounds him. Ahab was returned to Samaria, where he died, just as Micaiah had prophesied.

As you can see, these spirits are bold. They're bold enough to stand against you just like they stood up to answer God. Sometimes God will permit these spirits to come against you when you're disobeying God or, in my case, when he's trying to test your faith because I wasn't listening. These kinds of spirits are sneaky because they will use the prophets that sound innocent to steer you in the wrong direction. Or through our modern-day success messengers through the media or even someone close to you. These spirits know what you like and know what you want to hear. When God was speaking to me about his will for my life, I wasn't listening.

I only paid attention to what sounded good at the moment. So my name came up, and God permitted this same type of spirit into my life. Now did you notice how this spirit answered God? He said it would be easy to seduce him. I told you they've been watching you and your whereabouts all your life just like they've been watching Ahab and me. They know your every move just like they knew mine. This spirit knew I spent a lot of time on the media, he knew that I would visit other churches, and he knew what time of day I would tune into the radio. He studied how I thought and always knew how I felt about missing out on past opportunities, so he made his lies present everywhere my mind gave attention. If you don't know by now, you can convince your mind to believe anything if you consistently feed it the exact words. I know this, and the devil has known this since the beginning of humankind. So because my mind was being fed the same inspirations on social media, in churches through ministers, and motivations on the radio, of course, it was easy to seduce me over time. This same voice was speaking through multiple directions, and he could control my focus. In my mind, it was a positive thing as far as basketball, but the same tactics were used negatively. Everywhere you turn, its always something negative about your health. For example, If you're considered obese, this spirit will make sure everywhere you turn, you will see or hear about others who've died from overweight problems. He feeds your mind with worry and anxiety about the possibility of you being overweight, and the next thing you know, you're living life worrying about your death. That's why *"Jesus told you to pay attention to how you hear"* (Luke 8:18).

Our culture is filled with these spirits, and their territories have nearby tombs. The tombs represent your painful past experiences, whether physical, emotional, or death. Near the tombs, you will find familiar spirits and the people who associate with them. *"Let no one is found among you who sacrifices their son or daughter in the fire, practices divination or sorcery, interprets omens, engages in witchcraft, casts spells, or is a medium or spiritist or consults the dead. Anyone who does these things is detestable to the Lord"*(Deuteronomy 18:10-12). These spirits operate solely on whatever is familiar to you. Whether it is a deceased relative, a familiar addiction from your past, or what's familiar in your bloodline, these spiritists who consult the dead and read crystal balls or tarot cards operate in demonic realms. They're given access to these spirits to enter people's lives and not realize it. Have you ever heard someone say their deceased loved one visited them in their sleep? Well, I have, because I'm one of them. I had a dream where my stepfather visited me, but the problem was the background display. He showed up inside a tomb which was a "dead" giveaway as God revealed this was a familiar spirit around to torment me. They come around to try and keep you in that memorable sad place to keep you depressed. This man who was chained and often cut himself is the same person whose mind is stuck with a painful experience and constantly beats himself up. He can't get over past mistakes. He's the type of person who feels hopeless because he sees where the line was drawn through his generational name.

Day and night, he secretly cries out from this region of pain because someone has walked out of his life. No one could settle him because he had strength from the familiar and lying spirits. They both work together inside your family bloodlines and or family churches. I say it that way because I see it that way. When I break apart the word *'familiar,'* I see the words *'family' and 'liar'* within it. In other words, Lying spirits operate through your family on this side of your region. Jesus brought me on this site to understand all of this. The same region of your generational curse. The same region of your memories. The same region where the weapons form against you. It's an identical fight with something you can't see. It's where you've gotten lost trying to follow familiar images' footsteps. This region is where spiritual forces work against you, and some of these tactics I mentioned are how they stand in your way. What's familiar to you is also familiar to them, and they use it to their advantage.

The past failures and painful memories are all lying reminders to keep you chained near the tombs. Demons know Jesus is in front of this spiritual battle of names, and He wanted you to recognize what's been pulling from behind. But this chapter is over in your life, and it's time for you to get back into this relationship with God. He has a will for you, so pay attention while we return to the other side.

CHAPTER SIX
I Am Tussling Over Your Shirt

I entered the downtown area and circled around the squares. I dodged a few hanging tree limbs while parking out front. As I hopped down and slammed my door, I looked around at the high rises and continued to walk up the steps. Upon entering the double doors, I walked down the aisle towards the pulpit. My pastor shook my hand and guided me behind the podium. He stood behind me and asked, *"Am I ready"*? I proceeded to open my book and realized that my pen was missing. So I rushed down the aisle and exited to grab it out of my semi truck. Standing in shock, I realized that my truck was gone! I hesitated but turned around to head back inside. A portal of smoke enveloped around this whole scene and I immediately woke up. I stood up puzzled in bed and enventually grabbed my tablet to write down everything I saw. This was a personal vision from God that showed myself in the near future. In dreams and visions, it's important to remember everything including the smallest details. This vision showed where I was in life at the time and what I would be doing later. Most dreams you have in the night are usually forgotten when you're consciously awoke. But when it's from God, the image stamps into your mind and you will never be able to erase it. Visions and dreams is one way God will communicate with you. The Bible proves this accuracy of Him. To hear the voice of God, you must *"see"* what he is saying. Visions are like sign language to us and you must learn His language that's spoking. Two prophets in the Bible demostrates this best.

In Habakkuk 2:1-3; *"I will stand upon my watch, and set me upon the tower, and will watch to see what he will say unto me, and what I shall answer when I am reproved. And the Lord answered me, and said, Write the vision, and make it plain on clay tablets(books), that he may run that reads it. For the vision is yet for an appointed time, but at the end it shall speak, and not lie; though it tarry, wait for it; because it will surely come, it will not tarry."* I was in the middle of advancing my career and pursuing a dream of owning my own fleet. My life and heart was in order to accomplish it and I was beginning to figure out the ends and outs of the business world. Habakkuk prayed and was waiting to see what God would say about his concerns. Me on the other hand, wasn't praying at all but was busy arguing with this business life and God interrupted our back n forth disagreements. This vision showed that I was missing something, which was my pen for ministry. But as I went outside to look for it, my truck went missing. Yeah I wrote the vision down but I tucked it away and didn't care to look at it again. I wasn't trying to hear what God was saying to me once again but I never forgot what I saw. Jeremiah was another prophet who learned the sign language of seeing what God said. *"The word of the Lord came to me, saying, Jeremiah what do you see? Jeremiah 1:11."* Jeremiah recieved the call from God at a young age. He was no different from you when you were young. But God came to him early and showed him another image of himself. He said, *"Before I formed you in the womb I knew you, I have appointed you as a prophet to the nations."* Jeremiah wasn't sure about this vision like I wasn't sure. I was busy trying to figure out how I could develope my known field and God showed up with a landscape portrait of a new field. This was the beginning of my last chapter ending and we were now arriving into my new region.

From this day forward, it's a must that you forget about the last few chapter's of your life. This is the day that the Lord has made and you have arrived to your new beginnings. Get out and look at all the land around you. Look to the north, to the south, the east and the west. God calls you by your first name but you've been identifying by your whole name. Your 1st name represents this new region, this new country, and this new landscape. What I'm saying to you is, it's time for you to see your self image differently now. But I know that's easier said than done. Your new landscape is as beautiful as you can see it, it just needs a little work. Meaning, your inner landscape is the unconscious realm of your thoughts, emotions, memories, and beliefs that make up your psychological being. It's the sum total of all the experiences, feelings, and thoughts that you've accumulated over the last few chapters of life, and it was influencing the way you percieve and interact with the world around you. Trust me, I know this struggle very well. As a matter of fact, its been taking me awhile to hedge these old limbs and tossing all these weeds out. I've been working on this new land for years now. Most was wasted time just starring at it trying to see what in the world God sees but don't tell Him I admitted that to you. It's like, I remember him saying, *"I have a surprise for you back on the other side"*. And the next thing I know was this undeveloped land called *"a surprise"* in view. We arrived and I stood still on the beach side for awhile listening to his lectures. He kept encouraging me to explore more inland so He could help me gain a deeper understanding of my emotions, motivations, and behaviors. And the same is true with you. As we explore your inner landscape, you will identify patterns in your thinking and behavior that may be holding you back or causing you difficulties.

Jeremiah had difficulties as well. His name was called to set him apart from the society he was from. His message delivery was to the people of Israel, his own people, to confront the idolatry, wickedness, and impending judgements. His message clashed with the prevailing beliefs and practices of that time which isolated him with struggles and feelings of discouragements. His response to God was based on his self image of being young and inexperienced with speaking. (*"Then said I, Oh Lord God behold, I cannot speak; for I am a child said unto me. "But the Lord said unto me, Do not say, I Am a child: for thou shalt go to all that I shall send thee, and whatsoever I command thee thou shalt speak."* Jeremiah 1:6-7). These two verses show you how Jeremiah thought and how God thought, what Jeremiah had in his mind and what God had in mind. Sometimes what you have in mind for your in life is not the same direction God has in mind. As you can see, I had another direction I was traveling and God presented another map in my sight. When I looked at it again and observed the work that needed to be done, I looked at God and turned around towards the ship. I wanted to head back to the region I've known best. To me, the vision looked like I would end up public speaking somewhere and I wasn't comfortable with that. *"Who would want to hear what I have to say or read anything I ever write"*, was my thoughts walking away. But immediately the collar of my shirt was pulled back and God said, *"Be not afraid of their faces: for I AM with thee to deliver thee, said the Lord"*-(v. 8). My response to this pull was, *"Lord, see you don't understand, that's not who I am"*. It's the same response you think all the time when you pull away from God and this back n forth tussle between y'all has an underlining issue that needs to be addressed. It's knowing who I Am is and knowing who you are. In other words, this battle has now become you vs God.

God's response to you is *"I knew you before you were formed in the womb"*. But you don't know who I AM and you don't know who you are. You are a child of God, and because of that, you've learned to spiritually speak childish things. Jeremiah was correct when he spoke from a natural perspective but God corrected him spiritually. God said, *"do not say I AM a child"*, and what God is saying to you is, you need to understand who I AM. My name is *"I AM"* and it emphasizes my self-existence and eternal nature. It is derived from the Hebrew phrase *"ehyeh asher ehyeh"* meaning: I Am who I Am. I AM Alpha and Omega, the beginning and the end, the eternal and unchanging one. I AM your Redeemer who delivers and rescues you from slavery and sin. I AM your rock of refuge, stability, strength, and your firm fondation. I AM Elohim and El Shaddai, the Most High God with all power and might. Supremacy and sovereignty over all. I AM Jehovah-Jireh: The Lord who provides for you. I AM Jehovah-Rapha: The Lord who heals you and the source of all physical and spiritual restorations. I AM Jehovah-Shalom: Your source of peace and harmony. I AM Jehovah-Raah: The Lord who cares and directs you. I AM the Word, Jesus Christ, the incarnate word revealed to you in flesh. I AM the Comforter: the Holy Spirit who provides you comfort, guidance, and assistance on the inside of you. I Am Abba: your Spiritual Father who wants a intimate and loving relationship with you. And lastly, I AM fighting. Meaning, I'm fighting for you to believe in who I AM and who you are. Now what I Am not is *a child*! So I want you to say and have the right perspective of me Jeremiah(your name). I want you to know me for who I AM and I need you to believe who you are and who you're not. Now this is the beginning of the new journey so let's take a walk through your land and learn from some trails and areas of your nature.

The purpose of nature trails are the pathways to explore throughout the landscape of natural environments. The purpose of this book is for you to have a map to explore down the two trails of life ahead of you. The carnal trail and the spiritual trail. Both trails start off parallel to each other but eventually veers off. *"Those who live according to the flesh have their minds set on what the flesh desires; but those who live in accordance with the Spirit have their minds set on what the Spirit desires"* Romans 8:5. One trail leads to death, the other leads to life. The battle always comes when the paths start to veer off and you're force to make a split decision. *"The mind governed by the flesh is hostile to God; it does not submit to God's law, nor can it do so.-(v.7). "You, however, are not in the realm of the flesh but are in the realm of the Spirit, if indeed the Spirit of God lives in you. And if anyone does not have the Spirit of Christ, they do not belong to Christ(v.9). "The Spirit you recieved does not make you slaves, so that you live in fear again; rather, the Spirit you received brought about your adoption to sonship/daughtership. And by him we cry, "Abba, father" (v.15).*

I want you to understand that if and when you've accepted Christ, that two natures rises in your land. And because of that, you've just entered a lifetime of war. This war is all about who wins control over the land. The Spirit of God lives in you, but that part of you has just arrived to a undeveloped land. In other words, your flesh is governed by rugged law systems and you need to learn some differences about yourself. *"We know that the Law is spiritual, but I am a creature of the flesh(worldy, carnal and unspiritual), sold into slavery to sin (and serving under its control). For I do not understand my own actions. I do not practice what I want to do, but I am doing the very thing I hate(yeilding to my flesh nature). Now if I habitually do what I don't want to do, I agree with the Law, confessing that it is good. So now it is no longer I who do it, but the sin (nature) which lives in me. For I know that nothing good lives in me, that is, in my flesh. For the willingness (to do good) is present in me, but the doing of good is not. For the good that I want to do, I do not do, but I practice the very evil that I do not want. But if I am doing the very thing I do not want to do, I am no longer the one doing it (that is, it is not me that acts), but the sin nature which lives in me. So I find it to be the law (of my inner self), that evil is present in me, the one who wants to do good. For I joyfully delight in the law of God in my inner self(with my new nature), but I see a different law and rule of action in the members of my body(in its appetite and desires), waging war against the law of my mind and subduing me and making me a prisoner of the law of sin which is within my members"* **Romans 7:14-23. Paul was explaining the constant battle of the flesh and spirit. To help you understand this concept better, I want you to think about the nature of dogs. Dogs have unique behaviors and traits based on their upbringing, training, and individual personalities. The nature of a dog can be influenced by environmental factors and the specific breed or mix of breeds it belongs to. They are highly trainable, possess an innate ability to understand and respond to human commands. Picture your flesh as the image of a wild dog. It adapted to the environment and was free to roam around and get into** anything it felt the impulse to do. Now the dog in you became too aggressive over time and now has to be trained. It has to learn that a new master is alive and that new master is the real you. The dog's nature will fight against you because he's used to being free and doing things his way. He ate when he wanted to eat, whatever he felt like eating. That's right, he's responisble for your sweet teeth and over indulging appetites. He went places he felt led to go without any restraints. The dog in you was influenced by whatever environment was feeding him the most. The habitual behavior was strenghtened by the patterns he walked day to day. And you, who are alive spiritually, has to learn to control the two natures of you, and by deeply understanding the three distinctions of yourself.

Let's walk further into 1 Thessalonians 5:23. *"Now may the God of peace himself sactify you completely; and may your whole spirit, soul, and body be preserved blameless at the coming of our Lord Jesus Christ."* This verse suggests that they're three components to you. The spirit refers to the immaterial, eternal aspect of you. The possesion of your soul is the association of your mind, will, and emotions. Your body is only the physical and tangible aspect of yourself and you have to understand each part of you to understand the connections of the three components. The connection between your spirit and soul is described as closely intertwined. The Bible says the Word of

God is sharp like a double-edge sword that seperates spirit/soul like your bones and marrow. Your spirit is the eternal and divine aspect of yourself. This is the part of you that connects you to God and the spiritual realm. Your soul on the other hand, plays the role of a mediator between your spirit and body. The spirit part of you can influence the soul by providing guidance, inspiration while still connecting to God, while the soul responds through your thoughts, feelings, and decisions. Your soul is like the center of attention though. It's the most important part of you because it's also connected to your body. Your soul and body are what you and I most commonly associate with because of our earthly existence. The soul's thoughts, emotions, and wills are often expressed and experienced through your physical body. The body, in turn, can impact your soul through your five sensory experiences, physiological responses, and the limitations and natural abilities you possess. For example, bodily sensations can elicit emotional responses, and physical health or fatigue that can affect your mental and emotional states. You as a spiritual being, inhabit your body while you exists here on earth. Look at it this way, your body is like a bumper car to which your spiritual self experience and interact with the clashes of this physical world.

So you see how one aspect of yourself conflicts with the other. How the land externally, can effect you internally. Picture this nation of your flesh and the nature of the spirit rising in your own land. The two natures are like two nations in conflict over who has the most space to take over this land. We can explore more inland and you will see God ahead of you. He's in his word and he explains it best. Over in *"Genesis 25:23- And the Lord said, Two nations are in thy womb, and the two nations shall be seperated from thy bowels; and the one nation shall be stronger than the other nation; and the older shall serve the younger."* Rebekah was the wife of Isaac and was the first women to conceive a set of twins in the Bible. She obviously was experiencing internal struggles throughout her day to day life and sought God for some answers to why. To her suprise, God said she has two nations struggling within her. This struggle started internally and forshadowed a later conflict externally. The twins were Jacob and Esau. They both grew later to become fathers of nations. God knew all about this battle inside the womb before it ever existed outside between the two. God sees the same battle that resides in you and He's saying, *"one nation shall be stronger than the other nation, the older shall serve the younger"*. The older part of you is your fleshy nature that ruled your life but it will serve the spirit side of you. But in order for that to happen, a change has to take place. Jacob had a encounter with God and his name changed to Israel and he became the father of the 12 tribes of Israel. Esau's descendents on the other hand, were the Edomities. Edom was a nation that plagued Israel in later years and was finally judged by God. God seen the outcome of the undevelope land before the two nations existed. And he sees the outcome of your future before you existed. Despite your struggles, he knows how you grew up and he sees right through you like an open closet. Yeah, the dark space where you hang your skeletons in other words. In order for the change to happen, we have to open that closet and have a different perspective of what's hanging. As you know, skeletons in the closet has the meaning of a hidden life and secrets that you rather take to the grave. But God has a different meaning. The skeletons in your closet is what you hang on to and the label you wear everyday. Meaning, you don't feel good about yourself unless you advertise the label of other names. You've gotten caught up in the identity theft of names that are not even yours. Jacob had skeletons hanging in his closet and the time came for a change. He was going through life wearing a different label and God came and tussled over his shirt.

This story unfolds when Jacob is traveling back to his homeland after living with his uncle for years. As he nears his destination, he sends messengers ahead to his brother Esau, from whom he fled many years earlier due to their internal conflict. Jacob was concerned about Esau's reaction and is unsure if he will be received peacefully. Before crossing the river, Jacob sends his family and possessions across and remains alone on the other side. During the night in the wilderness, a mysterious man appears and begins to tussle with Jacob. This man was an Angel of God. This wrestling match continued throughout the night, with neither Jacob nor the Angel gaining the upper hand. As dawn approaches, the angel realizes he can't overpower Jacob and dislocates Jacob's hip with a blow.

However, Jacob continues to cling to the Angel and insists on recieving a blessing before letting him go. The Angel then asks Jacob his name, to which Jacob responds, and the Angel declares that his name will no longer be Jacob but Israel, which means *"one who struggles with God"*. Genesis 32:28. This renaming signified a change in Jacob's identity and his newfound status as the father of the twelve tribes of Israel. This whole tussle was over a name change. Jacob wore the label of a trickster and God snatched that shirt off for his future purpose. The labels you wear everyday is not a secret. You still wear the clothes of your affairs and you wear the cap of not being good enough. You hold on to the label of ADHD and you still try to lase your shoes of a criminal. You brought that shyness in XL and you dress fully in regrets. You stole all these identities to fit in your closet but God is about to pull on your shirt. The battle ignited when you learned to dress yourself back then. You brought these lies and figured the best way to mix and matched your outfits. Jacob learned the sameway. Even though he was a twin, he grew up different from Esau. Jacob was a quiet man, staying in the house close to his mom. She was his favorite. Esau was considered a skillful hinter, a man of the open country, and his father favorite. The division in the house was already taken place. So one day, Esau returned from hunting and desired some of the stew Jacob was cooking. Jacob offered to give his brother some stew in exchange for his birthright-the special honor that Esau possessed as the older son, which gave him the right to a double portion of his father's inheritance. Esau put his fleshy needs over his God-given blessing and sold his birthright to Jacob. That's a message in itself but this was one shirt labeled trickster in Jacob's closet. When the time came for Isaac to bestow his blessin on his sons, Jacob and his mother contrived to decieve Isaac into blessing Jacob in Esau's place. When Esau found out about his blessing was given to Jacob, he threatened to kill his brotheer, and this is why Jacob fled and was afraid in the future. So Jacob learned how to dress himself in manipulation as well from his mom. He basically stole the birthright and the blessing from his brother and was dressed in fear until God showed up to tear off that label.

You have a new identity and a new life to live now. God is tussling over your shirt because you're wearing something that was not made by him. Colossians 3:5-8 reads- *"Put to death, therefore, whatever in you is earthly: fornication, sexual impurity, evil passion and desires, and greed(which is idolatry). On account of these the wrath of God is coming on those who are disobedient. These are the ways you also once followed, when you were living that life. But now you must get rid of all such things-anger, wrath, malice, slander, and filthy language from your mouth."* Colossians 3:9-10 says, *"You're done with that old life. All of it is like a filthy set of ill-fitting clothes you've stripped off and put in the fire. Now get dress in your new wardrobe. Every item of your new way of life is custom-made by your Creator, with his label on it."* In other words, getting rid of your old wardrobe is letting go of every negativity and intentions from yesterday and throw it in the trash. It's like loosing the heavy weight of sin and working out the strenghts of your spirit. Forget about holding on to clothes that doesn't fit your spiritual frame now. God designed your own brand and he wants you to walk around advertising what he put in you. You also have brand new shoes that is fitted for you. This whole wardrobe is hanging in the corner of your closet and what you need to do is open up to see what you have. God pulled on my shirt because it was time for me to change. The conflict was the hestitation of not being sure of myself. Walking back inside that church was like walking out the path ahead of me that I couldn't see. The only trail I seen revolve around my pen to write. The pulling of you is because you need to change. The path is there but you must turn to see it. It's a new thinking pattern that you need to walk in and it starts with the vision he will show you. The vision of myself showed that I had shoes that was customed designed in a box with my name on it. And right now I'm walking in them and I'm starting to break them in. The vision God gives you will be uncomfortable at first. He says we walk by faith and not by sight for a reason, its taking steps towards the vision. He's going to show you a undeveloped land that belongs to you. You have something fitted for you to explore through this new land.

Taking a step of faith is mastering the next step it takes for you to accomplish this new path infront of you. He has a new career, a new ministry, a new relationship and a new destination in view for you. But it requires you to strip yourself from your past thinking, fears, and your past doubts. The I AM God is starring right at you and He's tugging on you and pointing you foward.

CHAPTER SEVEN
Your Dash Is Digital

As I continued to walk alongside God, we came upon the entrance of a cemetery. I was thinking to myself, *"So what now?"* I observed the perfectly mowed grass and the bundled flowers placed beside the graves while we continued toward the back. Before we could reach the fence, I noticed an open box beside a freshly dug grave. It must have been at least noon, but nobody was in sight. It was complete silence around me while I stood puzzled. To me, it looked like someone knew exactly what was in there, and they knew the exact spot to find it. But then the Spirit spoke. He said, "Pay Attention because this is a lesson about you!" If you think your earthly father taught you difficult lessons, wait until God comes in. It always seems like a lesson you'd rather avoid. This is Erie to me, and why are we here, Lord? He said it's two lessons I want you to learn from this. You've observed the empty box already, but I was hoping you could look at your tombstone and tell me what you see. I took a good look at it and immediately woke up.

Before we dive deeper into this, I want to make sure you're clear about all this. I pointed out in the last chapter that you, as a spiritual being, can connect with God with your Spirit. And your Spirit can answer the questions God asks while you're in deep slumbers. One of the proofs I have for you is King Solomon, the wealthiest man ever known. In 1 King chapter 3:5-15, God came to Solomon in his dream and said, *"Ask for whatever you want me to give you."* Solomon said, *"You've shown great kindness to your servant, my father David, because he was faithful to you, righteous and upright in heart. You have continued this great kindness to him and given him a son to sit on his throne today. Now, Lord, you have made your servant king in place of my father, David. But I'm only a child and don't know how to carry out my duties. Your servant is here among the people you've chosen, too numerous to count. So give me a discerning heart to govern your people and to distinguish between right and wrong. For who can govern this great people of yours? The Lord was pleased and said; since you've asked for this instead of long life and wealth for yourself, nor have you asked for the death of your enemies, I will do what you've asked. I will give you a discerning heart so that there will never have been anyone like you, nor will there ever be. Moreover, I will give you what you haven't had yet to ask for wealth and honor- so that you will have no equal among kings in your lifetime. And if you walk in obedience to me and keep my commands as David, your father, did, I will give you a long life. Then Solomon woke up and realized it had been a dream".* **So you see, Solomon and God were communicating back n forth through the Spirit, and the evidence of that conversation was seen throughout Solomon's waking life.**

This is important for you to know because this is part of your ability............... Now it's common to hear a sermon about dashes at funerals. From sunrise to sunset, we've heard it many times, but that kind of message is supposed to make you think about yourself. These type of messages helps you to focus on what's important and what you did do with your time on earth. I'm confident that you're somewhere in the middle of your dash because you're blessed to be reading this book. But I want to give you another perspective because it's something special about you and your dash. This vision I was in showed two lessons I had to learn and the first dealt with this empty box. This dream meant something in me was buried deep and is now out in the open. The person who dug it up was God, with no one else around to see it. This became mysterious to me because where on earth would I start to hunt for what was missing in me?

But the tombstone was the clue. The dash was the focal point and had something to do with time. So I prayed, *"Lord, I need a lifeline because I'm clueless over here."* He said what was in your box was an ability you possess, and it's connected to something you loved in your past; the dash is your clue. As I meditated on the word *"dash,"* the only thing that popped up was running and racing. Like running a 40-yard dash or something. I never loved running like that because I was slow as a baby, so I knew that couldn't be it. But as I thought more on it, running, racing, and 40-yard dashes all have something to do with speed. And this is when the lightbulb is switched on. The love I had for riding my sports bike was a life dead to me, but what does that have to do with something I possess in the open now?

In your youth, it was nothing for you to wake up from bed and hit the ground running. The energy stored up gave you a boost when it was time to run and play outside. It was all fun and games, especially if you enjoyed racing. Now I was slower than some of my friends when it came to running, but the competition was on for riding bikes. I wasn't paying attention to how my body worked together then, but I've learned some things now. Running and riding a bike have something in common: the power of your muscles being used. Both require much energy and strength depending on the time, speed, and distance. If I compare the two in a short-distance race, the person running on foot will beat a person on a bicycle simply because of the take-offs. Initially, the runner is lighter than someone holding up a bike. Therefore, he accelerates quicker. But let's say I stretched the distance from a 20-yard dash to a 100-yard dash; the bike rider easily wins. His takeoff is much slower because his energy and strength are transmitted from his muscles to the pedals and gears of the bicycle, but with the distance, he catches up quickly. Now both racers have experience in burnout, but a runner will experience it much sooner. Because he's using his whole body to run a race, he has limits to his capabilities.

On the other hand, the bike rider has an advantage, but he still needs more muscle strength with the distance. Even though he has the mechanical help of a bike, his muscle stamina is still needed for further distances. You can pick up where I'm going with this. Your takeoff speed in life was no different. You had all the energy and strength to compete with anybody at the beginning of your life. But as you've gotten older, the distance seemed like a stretch, and your energy started to change. Your life is like this race. Meaning when you were in your school years, life looked like fun n games outside of the house, but the day you picked up that bicycle called *"work,"* your energy started to shift. The 100-yard dash of life resembled a 9-5 marathon in the distance. The day-in and day-out jobs became exhausting because of the rising living cost. I have some scars and bruises showing up on my bank account and my credit report from the falls I experienced from this exhaustion. How many times did I switch bikes to get quicker results?

My resume is like a receipt of my bicycle purchases from a toy section. And I'm not ashamed to admit that. I'm grown but still acted childish because I constantly desired to swap for a fancier bike. But I realized no bike was much different from the other, and I was wasting time. So as of now, my kickstand is down, and I've taken a break from racing to talk with you. I'm looking around and noticing some people are not here with us in this marathon. One of the reasons for this is how we've been trained to run. Times have changed, and we've been trained like a child to use our muscles the most to beat the cost, like working on machines and using physical labor on jobs. All of it uses up our energy, and we eventually burn out. But competition is rising, and the race could be more fun. You are now in a race competing with technology and machines that cycle independently. And traditional pedaling is going to take a bit longer. We're reaching our limits, and it's time to upgrade to something stronger and much faster for this race.

You have to upgrade to a faster bike to experience similar fun and play outside of life. The one that requires muscle, use of your hands, and mind. This is where the love of motorcycles comes into play. What you physically could do with your heart and legs can't compare to what you can mentally do with your heart and hands. The burnouts are a lil different when it comes to motorcycles, which means the rubber is burning on the road before a quick takeoff. For example, sports bikes are known for their high-performance capabilities and power. The impressive accelerations come from powerful engines and lightweight frames that can go from 0 to high speeds in seconds, delivering a thrilling burst of speed and adrenaline. The acceleration is controlled by your hand twisting the throttle. The aerodynamic design and streamlined fairings help reduce wind resistance, allowing you as a rider to achieve and maintain high velocity. The advanced suspension system and high-performance tires featured on a responsive chassis contribute to exceptional handling and agility. This allows you to navigate corners and curves with precision and confidence, depending on the skill set of your hand and mind. Sport bikes often have a power-to-weight ratio, meaning they have considerable horsepower about their weight. The ratio enhances their performance, as the power generated by the engine is effectively utilized to propel the bike forward. They're also track-ready performance. Meaning they're designed with race tracks in mind. The technology and designed elements are borrowed to provide you with a similar experience to professional racers. Motorcycles and sports bikes are basically programmed for high-rated speeds. It's usually noticed on the speedometer on how fast it can go. But even though it's built that way, it can only reach that potential with you. The motorcycle needs the hand and mind of someone to push it to its limit, and this is where I come in.

The beginning of my ridings days was exciting. I've learned the basics of balancing the weight while walking the bike in a straight line, to taking off in 1st and shifting to 2nd gear in a parking lot. When I got used to that, my next step was shifting to higher speeds in traffic. I could maneuver around the city safely on my own, but the time came for me to ride with a group. Let me tell you something; if you want to experience the fun of riding bicycles with your buddies down the street again, try joining a motorcycle club as an adult. Big boys still have big toys they enjoy, and this was an experience I always remember. I'll never forget the first night I rode with everybody. We always met at a neutral point, store, or someone's house and planned our night ride. One of the guys said, *"I guess we'll open 'em up tonight."* The plan was to cross the state line and have some wings at a bike night event. It sounded like a plan to me, and I was excited but didn't realize I was the rookie of the pack and what we'll open them up meant. I said that because we had to ride on the interstate, but I only had experience within the city limits. And I thought I was doing something when we pulled off by racing to the front of the pack. But as we veered on the interstate ramp, I couldn't accelerate past 62mph. Cars and semi-trucks flew by, and some guys maneuvered to the fast lane and shot off like rockets. Blue flames proceeded out their exhaust pipes, and all I could see were red dots vanishing out of sight.

I was struggling to keep up, and the curves made it worst. I became terrified of the learning involved, and about 15 minutes later, I finally pulled up last and felt embarrassed. I asked, *"Man, how fast was ya'll going"*? One guy responded, *"I hit about 185mph"*....... 185!...... That's what they meant by opening them up as I shook my head. I knew then that I had a lot more riding to do because the bike wasn't the problem; I was. My hand and mind would not let me accelerate past 62, and I've started to learn why. For one, I was practicing within the city limits, and two, I needed to learn the real capabilities of my own bike. That 185 amazed me so much that I made my personal goal exceed that. I wanted to see myself as a real bike rider and push past their limit, but the problem with that is the speedometer on my dash was digital. The glow of digital numbers appeared only as I picked up speed, so I was suspicious of how fast I could go. This is the principle I want to teach because my dash, your dash, and my bike dash has no visible limits.

Now because it's a sports bike, I committed to the goal of reaching an even number of 200mph. I had a powerful bike back then. It was a 2006 suzuki gsxr 1000cc, and I knew it could reach those speeds. The capacity was designed within the bike, but I had to be the one to push it to the limits. Your dash is digital because your life is digital. You are like the image of a sports bike, and God designed you with invisible limits. Meaning you can't visibly see your high-rated lifestyle. You were built with high capacities to handle all the curves of life ahead easily. But the problem is that your mind does not allow you to twist your throttle more than your limits. I'll give you an illustration of what I mean. You and I practiced within the city limits, and this represents our labored jobs. For 365 days, we dashed around the city limits, earning an average of around $50,000 annually. And this continued year after year of you hoping for an increase to beat the rising costs. Your job is like the posted speed limit signs around the city that you operate in, and you're only limited to 50mph. So you've got accustomed to barely *getting by* other vehicles of your life. But you have the capability to reach $200,000 in the same year. And that represents the goal I had in mind to reach 200mph. So you've built with the potential of 200, but you're comfortable at 50 until the boys say, "It's time to open 'em up"! The life you've been living doesn't have to be exhausting anymore because you have something else available. It's the potential of your hand and mind connection, but that needs to be challenged. In other words, it's time to break some speeding laws. I knew to reach my goal of 200mph, and I had to push my limits. It's a lesson I'm mastering right now as I speak. My motorcycle experience has principles God wanted me to recognize and share with you. I've realized how powerful the mind is because I couldn't just jump out on the highway and speed up to 200; my mind wouldn't let me. But I took some initiative to push to 90. 90mph on two wheels is fast. Just think about all the wind hitting me all at once. Now my mind is battling the wind and the thought of police clocking me over the speed limit. So I got used to reaching 90 from 0 quickly while I embraced the winds and held my balance.

The next goal was to reach 110mph. Those speeds didn't feel much different, but my mind forced me to back off the triple-digit thoughts. I still was a long way from 200, but I started to get comfortable and have fun in these triple digits. That's what 6 figure income feels like, huh? Comfortable and having fun. Now, my hand and mind connected without resistance, and I didn't fear police clocking me. My confidence was boosted because I efficiently handled the bike and was familiar with its capacity. I knew they couldn't catch me, is my point. But I'm pointing all this out to say the invisible speed limits in my mind were broken, and I learned to operate outside these limits. The joy wasn't felt inside the city limits as it was on the freeway; the same feeling can be felt through your hand and mind connections.

Can you imagine a city with no limits? If vehicles can operate as fast as it was designed, how would that look in the traffic of life? To me, it will look like freedom despite what you think about safety. I reason that because your mind is never trained to operate within limits governed by a man. Now you can go as slow or fast as you want, but the option should be up to you. That's freedom to me, and that's how God wants us to be free. God never set limits on us; man designed that. How does a man program you to live inside limits when God built you past them? Or how does a job tell you you're worth when God created you for more? God has a place in life just for you and has no limits. This place is like the Autobahn in Germany. The autobahn is a system of highways known for its sections that have no general speed limits. It's famous for being one of the few places in the world where drivers can legally travel at high speeds. The autobahn is a symbol of German engineering prowess and is often associated with the concept of unrestricted speed and driver freedom. Freedom comes when restrictions are broken in your mind, and you're built to break them. But you need someone to come along and show you how. Breaking free from the restrictions and limits of your mind is like breaking free from systems of prisons. And here's an example for us to learn from. In the book of Acts, Peter was inside a prison awaiting trial.

At the time, King Herod Agrippa persecuted the early Christian community in Jerusalem. He had James, the brother of John, put to death, and seeing that this pleased the Jews, he proceeded to arrest Peter as well. Acts 12:4-10 says, *"And when he had apprehended him, he put him in prison, and delivered him to four guards to keep him; intending after the Passover to bring him forth to the people. Peter, therefore, was kept in prison, but prayer was made without ceasing of the church unto God for him. And when Herod would have brought him forth, the same night, Peter was sleeping like a baby between two guards, bound with two chains: the keepers before the door kept the prison. And suddenly, the Angel of the Lord came upon him, and a light shined in prison: and he smote Peter on the side, and raised him, saying, Rise up quickly. And his chains fell off his hands. And the Angel said unto him, Gird thyself, and bind on thy sandals. And so he did. And saith unto him, Cast thy garment about thee and follow me. And he went out, and followed him; and couldn't believe it was true which was done by the Angel, but he thought it was only a vision. When they passed the first and second guard, they came unto the iron gate that leads unto the city, which opened to them on its own: and they went out, and passed on through one street: and then the Angel departed from him."* **I represent this Angel right now because I'm showing up inside your mental prison system and have a message from God. He says,** *"I have a place designed just for you that has no limits to your capabilities, but I see you're hands are chained, and your mind is incarcerated. You've been working for the world long enough, and I need you to escape this old lifestyle and follow me out. Do not fear being caught by the system because they aren't powerful enough to catch up to you."* **To experience this great escape, I need you to Rise Quickly! In other words, It's time for you to** *"open 'em up."*

You have built-in gifts and potential that have something to do with your hands and mind. Opening them up is searching for what's missing in your life. You're not satisfied and enjoying life because you're only operating within the laws of systems. You grew up in a system of schools, you grew up in a system of religion, you grew up in a system of jobs, and all of these learned systems are set and designed for the general population. It's nothing against any of these because we all need a starting point to accelerate, but it's time to pick up your speed. Your throttle is what brings you joy and happiness when your hand and mind connect with your gifts. Stop being lazy in your thoughts and maneuver in the fast lane of your life. You know within yourself that you can do more than what you've been doing. You're allowing technology to replace your creativity, and you're asleep with abilities. It makes you glow, and you know exactly what it is. Only you and God can see that.

This glow is like the glow on my dash when I crunk up for a night ride. As I turned the key, my dashboard became lit with high-speed potential, and I was ready to break some laws. I became courageous over time because I recognized the power I had in my hand. I learned how to control my bike and realized it was possible to reach my 200mph goal. One night, I decided to test my hands and mind. We were all pulling out from a bike night event and cruised towards the expressway. We approached the intersection that opened up to it, and this was the starting point for each of us to head home. We all looked around while revving our engines, waiting for the green light. Shields down, tires burning out, and the take-off happened. It's about midnight, but our bikes are screaming and yelling in the fast lanes. Two lanes eventually widened to three, and that's when it was time to open them up. I crouched down to hug my bike and shot past some cars like a rocket. When I cleared past the few cars, I said to myself, *"Rise up quickly"*! I twisted my throttle, held it down, and my eyes experienced tunnel vision. I switched my bright lights on as the lanes started to close in on me. Seconds later, I quickly glanced at my dash, and it read 185mph. This whole experience has principles to what Peter experienced in prison. This Angel showed up as this bright light in the cell. The same glow I had on my dash at night. He instructed him to *"rise up quickly,"* and the chains fell off. I came a long way from 62mph, but I learned to accelerate quickly past the speed limits that trained my mind to abide by. And the fact that he couldn't believe he was following an Angel right out of the prison that led him to the opening of an iron gate shows his tunnel vision. I've seen how tunnel vision looked in movies, but I couldn't believe I was experiencing it myself. Tunnel vision is about focusing on your mind's eye and what you're doing with your hands. You know you're speeding past your limits when nothing outside of you is distracting. Once locked in your own lane, this will lead you towards the iron gate of your city, where you thrive.

With this experience, I can admit to not reaching the 200mph mark. Again, my mind wouldn't allow it because of fear and comfort. Yes, I reached 185, but my mind only witnessed that possibility from the other riders. I had never heard or seen anyone else do what I wanted to accomplish, so guess what? My mind was limited to that 185 mark. Do you see how powerful the mind is? I've heard many voices in the land preach that kind of message, but I've experienced that revelation through my bike. I was allowing my hand and mind to be limited only by what I saw with my natural eyes. And because of that, I was missing out on the thrills of my potential inside the city limits. This has taught me a valuable lesson about life. God designs us but we can be programmed by the world. And the dash on your tombstones will reveal the limits that you lived in. I'm not speaking from a place of rushing through life, but I am speaking from a place of making the most out of your life. You only have one race to run, so you can open up and push past the limits. You're in the middle of your dash right now, and God has already drugged up your box, and something deep in you is out.

When you find what's missing, you will find your joy, you will find your fulfillment, and you will find yourself. This ability to write and teach in books was in me all the time. This is one of my hand and mind's creative gifts with the hidden potential to reach higher speeds. This is not limited because what I'm doing now will outlive me. That's a clue for your dash in life, but it's invisible. Meaning your dash is digital because you have the potential to do something more significant that will live past you. You're used to making a living, but it's time for you to make a difference. But if you don't take that walk with God and review your mind from that old dead life, you won't notice that potential missing. I witness him speaking in the Spirit like Solomon and trust that he will visit you soon. And when he does, ask him to open up what's missing in you.

CHAPTER EIGHT
Discover Your Identity

I opened my eyes and noticed two Beechcraft King Air 360s idling on the runway. As I walked toward one of the jets, I stopped and looked around. I was in the middle of nowhere, and all that was around were snow-covered mountains. After takeoff, we climbed as high as the Earth's atmosphere, but then we started to descend. I spoke out loud, saying, *"I wanna go higher"*! Immediately the aircraft tilted back, and an explosion sounded off as I crossed into space. The next thing I noticed was my wife on the phone and hanging up clothes in the closet. My father-in-law was decorating a Christmas tree, and a voice commanded me to turn around. We were inside a house, and a T.V. was on a stand by the window with Earth showing on the screen. Out of curiosity, I peeked out the curtains and was astonished that I'd arrived on the moon. In my view, Earth appeared more straightforward outside the window, and I woke up and wrote this vision down...

In the book of Joel, there is a scripture that talks about dreams and visions. It's found in Joel 2:28-29: *"And afterward, I will pour out my Spirit on all people. Your sons and daughters will prophesy, your old men will dream dreams, and your young men will see visions. Even on my servants, both men, and women, I will pour out my Spirit in those days."* This passage in the Old Testament is a prophecy about the Holy Spirit. It speaks of a future time when God's Spirit will be poured out on all people, resulting in various manifestations such as prophesying, dreaming, dreams, and seeing visions. It emphasizes that this pouring out of the Spirit will not be limited by age, gender, or social status but will be available to all who seek God.

We live in these future times of this particular prophecy, and I'm one of the living witnesses. My spiritual eyes opened in this vision to enlighten me on the season I was in. The fact that the mountains were covered with snow and my family members were decorating the tree reminded me of the Christmas season, the time of year when we acknowledge the birth of Christ and the season of giving gifts. At this moment, I was entering this season of identity and experiencing it in H.D. The Spirit poured out on me and presented a visual gift that provided a higher visual quality with sharper and more detailed images. The turning-around instruction was to repent of my old life and recognize the surprise gift. In other words, God gave me a t.v. for Christmas that wasn't wrapped. And the only way I could see it was from me traveling higher in the Spirit. You will notice certain things about your real identity once you climb higher in the Spirit. In the New Testament, John is my other witness of this outpouring of God's Spirit. He wrote the book of Revelation, which interprets *"The Revelation of Jesus Christ"* as the book's title. The revelation is both from Christ and about Christ. Since Christ is the revelation of God Himself, God gave the revelation to Christ to be shown to John through an angel. (Revelation 1:1). John also witnessed what he wrote. God gave him visions and commanded him to write them in this book. This same author, John, wrote the Gospel of John and was blessed to record his experiences with Jesus twice. In the flesh, as he walked with Jesus, and in the Spirit, through the visions of Jesus. In Revelation 4:1-2, John wrote a similar experience of what I'm communicating with you. It reads, *"After this, I looked, and, behold, a door was opened in heaven: and the first voice I heard was of a trumpet talking with me; which said, Come up here, and I will show thee things to come. And immediately I was in the Spirit: behold, a throne was set in heaven, and one sat on the throne."*

John was on the rocky island of Patmos in the Aegean Sea when he wrote this book. The similarity is that this door was down, and he boarded his spiritual plane and climbed into the heavenly realms. When he arrived, he heard this authoritative voice saying, *"Come closer because I have something for you."* As we know it, this surprise was the revelation of God's throne, and he recorded everything in detail that he saw. But the point I want you to see is the ticket he had and what was waiting for him upon his arrival.

You see, you have a ticket that's available for you to get access to heaven. And this ticket is paid in full for you to approach this luxurious jet in wait for you. It's a spiritual jet I want your eyes to see, and some experiences and lessons come with this flight. On John's Spiritual Jet, he experienced some high altitudes and turbulences that he recorded in his book for us to study. Similarly, I have some Spiritual Jet experiences as well. I want to take you on a quick journey in the atmosphere and teach you what's been shown to me. As you know, a plane is a designed vehicle for transporting people through the air, but this ticket is not for you to experience my hospitality, but for the cockpit.

Now I was blessed to circle the Sun 35 times and wake up to get dressed for a huge surprise. After we left the house, I was blindfolded as I rode down the highway. Upon our arrival, the blindfold was snatched off, and I stood in front of my county airport. I held on to a desire to fly for a while, but my wife decided to surprise me with a paid-in-full ticket. Now listen, Before you enroll in flight school, you must take a discovery flight first. And since I never flew on an airplane a day in my life, I expected my mind to back out of this. But my Spirit was able to overcome my anxious thoughts. So the discovery flight is exactly what it sounds like. If you desire to do anything in life, I encourage you to get into the atmosphere of people and the environment of your desires first. You need to see and feel what it's like to live in this space before you commit to this journey. Your passion has to burn more than the obstacles you will face ahead, and that's what the discovery flight is all about. My first time flying was about to begin in the cockpit seats, and this was an experience to remember. A lot of principles as well.

After I signed my paperwork, we headed out back, where the fleet of planes was all tied down. We proceeded with the pre-flight checklist to detect any safety issues and taxied around the airport toward the takeoff strip. Before takeoff, we needed to radio the control towers because of air traffic. Now the skies looked clear, but I couldn't see what they saw in the air, so we stood still until further notice. The tower gave us clearance, and we got into position for takeoff. It got real for me because the instructor engaged the engine with more thrust, and the propellers made it feel like we wanted to levitate. I then realized that the power of this aircraft was built for the air and not the ground. So he released the brakes, and we thrust down the runway until we picked up enough speed to pull the lever back. The feelings from this takeoff were experienced in two different ways.

My mind could detect the speed on the ground, but my thoughts shifted as we climbed into the air. There were no obstacles to compare our speed in the air, so I felt like we were ballooning. I asked him how fast we were going, and he smirked, saying, *"110 knots"*. The first thing I thought was, how can some people say the world is flat ground? The higher we soared, the more rounded Earth appeared in the distance. I was trying to relax while I watched life problems left down there, but we started to hit invisible speed bumps, which made me nervous. I looked at him and asked, *"Is this supposed to happen?"* Again, he smirked and started to explain what was going on that I didn't understand. He explained that the aircraft was not designed to fall out of the sky, and I had nothing to worry about. Even if the engine fails, we still have control because of the body frame and how the wings were built. He even encouraged me to take control and feel what it's like to fly. The instrument panels have attitude and altitude readings, and I took control for about 10 seconds. For 10 seconds, I was controlling my destiny. I was the pilot of my life, and I felt what it was like to be in control in a different atmosphere. But I quickly handed that back over to the professional. As we learned in the last chapter, my mind said, *"That's enough!"* So, as we continued to soar around the landscape, our destination was in view. This was when my mind shifted back to reality. We were approaching the landing strip, and I noticed all the preparations that took place for landing safely—slowing the plane down for one and contacting the towers again. The lower we descended, the faster we seemed to be going. Because now life obstacles were around, and my mind could judge our speeds. I felt like I wanted to hold my breath until our wheels finally made contact with the asphalt. We immediately slowed down, and everything was back to normal as we headed back toward the building. We discussed my plans to move forward with training because he felt that I was ready for the skies. He said most people think they want to pursue something like this until they get in the air. He had people faint and even puke on him when they realized what flying in the cockpit was really like. So I noted that to encourage you to do the same with your dreams.

After discovering flight, the next step was to learn aerodynamic wisdom from their books. Training started with the wisdom of aircraft books and what they're made for. If you ever want to find wisdom for anything, look at the purpose of everything around you, and you will find some. But the best place to start searching is in books. Books are the best place to find wisdom because wisdom is broken down in detail. John started by giving us God's wisdom from the beginning of time. *"In the beginning was the word, and the word was with God, and the word was God. The same was at the beginning with God. He made all things, and without him, was not anything made that was made. In him was life, and the life was the light of men. And the light shineth in darkness; and the darkness comprehended it not."* (John 1:1-5) These verses parallel the beginning of Genesis, when God created the universe. God created everything we see in 6 days and rested on the 7th. Each day provides wisdom for us to learn something, but I want to concentrate on the 4th day. The verse says: *"And God said, Let there be lights in the firmament of the heaven to divide the day from the night; and let them be for signs and seasons. and for days and years: And let them be for lights in the firmament of the heaven to give light upon the Earth, and it was so. And God made two great lights, the greater light to rule the day, and the lesser light to rule the night: he made the stars also. And God set them in the firmament of the heaven to give light upon the Earth, rule over the day and night, and divide the light from the darkness: and God saw that it was good."*(v.14-18). God left some details for us to learn from, just like my trip to the moon.

The greater and lesser light spoken refers to the Sun and moon. Representing the celestial bodies in heaven and the spiritual realm. On the other hand, Earth is the terrestrial body, and our fleshly bodies are an image of our physical realm. Life is in God, and God is Spirit. And that life is the light of men which shines in darkness on Earth. We live in this darkness until the Sun shines on us in the Earth. And this light is a direct image of where God's wisdom comes from. For better understanding, here's some wisdom God showed me from the moon or in the Spirit. God provides wisdom for us to heal naturally from any sickness. Because our flesh was made from the Earth, we must reflect its image and listen to what it says. If you look at the Earth, the colors and movement instruct you how to live longer. Green and blue are all the colors you see, representing veggies and water our bodies need. But the Earth spins on its axis to show and teach us how we should exercise daily. If you're considered overweight, consider how your body and health would transform in 365 days of eating fruits and vegetables and drinking water. With a 20-minute walk or jog every day for a year, you will become a brand new person after your trip around the Sun. Do you hear wisdom speaking? The Earth is consistent with her diet and light exercise; it speaks wisdom to you. The celestial bodies are no different. They both speak wisdom for us to learn spiritual insights. The image of the Sun, moon, and stars first teaches us their positions. They're ranked at a higher level of the kingdom of heaven. The kingdom of heaven is like the kingdom of the air; they both teach us invisible principles. There are invisible laws that exist in the heavens, and we're familiar with the lower ones. We're familiar with things we can see, like airplanes that abide by the principles of aerodynamics. It involves studying how air behaves around objects and motion through the air. Newton's law of motion plays a fundamental role in aerodynamics.

The three laws-namely, the law of inertia, the relationship between force and acceleration, and the principle of action and reaction, explain how forces interact with objects in motion. These laws govern the forces of thrust, lift, drag, and weight that act on any aircraft. Throughout the years, this wisdom was taught from the image of birds. I told you, each created day has wisdom for us to learn. Whoever thought we would see transportation through the wisdom of birds. Birds not only taught us the laws of flight, but they're also the direct image of spirits. Jesus was baptized in the Jordan River, and John the Baptist saw the Holy Spirit descend on him like a dove. Jesus also explains parables about the kingdom of heaven. He said it's like a man who sowed seeds on the ground, but the birds swooped down to steal the seeds. Or the kingdom of heaven is like a mustard seed that grew to be the tallest tree in the forest where birds' nests are built. Doves and birds are all referred to as these spirits. The Holy Spirit and also these evil spirits steal the word from your heart and build nests on your head. Catch some of this wisdom spoken by Jesus. The Bible speaks about some angels with wings, and birds reflect these angels' images. All three of these examples have one thing in common, though, and that's the wings to fly. Wings are designed to fly by the kingdom's rules, and the wings represent the gift for the environment. The wings of a bird are designed for the air and not the nest. The same is true about airplanes. The wings are designed for balance in the air and not to be tied to the ground. No wonder the levitation was felt as we exerted more power on the engine. But the reason for the tie-downs is for strong winds of storms. Because it's built for the air, it will easily levitate with strong gusty winds, and we wouldn't want planes just floating around and tumbling through your neighborhood.

Now when you notice a gift like these wings, you should be able to discern environments. Meaning, look for all the wisdom around it. Your environment may reveal your gifts or vice versa. The celestial bodies give you the wisdom of their gifts and environments. Their light is the gift, and space is their environment to shine that gift for us. God said, Sun, I need you to rule this space on the day shift, and moon, I need you to rule the night shift. The moon gives us hope for something greater to come that we can't see in the dark. It is the light of the world, reflecting the sustaining life for a man to live off. The moon also reflects the Sun from the other side, but it has to be in the proper position and environment for us to see. In other words, it represents God's word and wisdom through the Bible. This same wisdom is for you to recognize your space in life to rule using your spiritual gifts. Your environment and gifts will direct you to your space of rulership, but you have to discover it.

The best way to start is by looking *"up"* at the word and noticing what's there. Paul wrote Timothy encouraging him to stir up the gifts God gave him. But to stir up your gifts, you must notice what's there. Spiritual gifts are listed in Romans 12, 1 Corinthians 12, 1 Peter 4, and Ephesians 4. Romans and 1 Corinthians list the same gifts, but more are listed in Corinthians. *"Now there are varieties of gifts, but the same Spirit; and there are varieties of services, but the same Lord; and there are varieties of activities, but the same God who empowers them all in everyone. Each is given the manifestation of the Spirit for the common good. For to one is given through the Spirit the utterance of wisdom, and another the utterance of knowledge according to the same Spirit, to another faith by the same Spirit, to another gift of healing by the one Spirit, the working of miracles, to another prophecy, to another the ability to distinguish between spirits, to other various kinds of tongues, to another the interpretation of tongues. All these are empowered by the same Spirit, who apportions to each one individually as he wills.*"(1 **Corinthians 12:4-11). Romans 12 lists gifts of prophecying, serving, teaching, encouraging, giving, leadership, and mercy. And in Ephesians 4, this list of gifts refers to the office space given to you to perform your functions inside God's church, which means the members of the body of Christ, not the church buildings per se.** *"There is one body, and one Spirit, even as ye are called in one hope of your calling; one Lord, one faith, one baptism, one God and Father of all, who is above all, and through all, and in you all. But unto every one of us is given grace according to the measure of the gift of Christ. Wherefore he saith, When he ascended on high, he led captivity captive And gave gifts unto men. Now that he ascended, what is it but that he descended first into the lower parts of the Earth? He that descended is the same as ascending far above all heavens that he might fill all things. And he gave some apostles; and some, prophets; and some, evangelists; and some pastors and teachers; for the perfecting of the saints, for the work of the ministry, for the edifying of the body of Christ."***(Ephesians 4:4-12). In other words, God is saying,** *"my child(your name), I present to you the door of your office. This is your cockpit, and I need you to draw up a creative plan to serve and better the world. You have enough space to rearrange what's necessary for you to get the job done. Go in, look around, and use the functions that are available to you. Once you're seated, you will easily see what I'm talking about. I left 66 books of wisdom in the back for more guidance. I'll keep in* *touch with you to check on your progress."* ....Sitting in the seat of an Apostle, Prophet, Evangelist, and dual Pastor/Teacher is considered the office of a church. You and God will always communicate through the towers, discussing your route and assignments in this world. He gives you creatively say so in the preplan, as long as you're clear on where you sit.

The books available are for you to understand your functions in detail. For instance, 1 Peter 4:9-11 divides the gifts into two as if workers are divided into shifts. One shift is for speaking, telling stories, teaching, directing, or anything that involves your voice. This is the Ephesians 4 office gifts category, and your primary job is to speak. The other shift is for ministering and support—anything to do with serving, helping, and encouraging the people. Your primary shift could involve using multiple gifts, but I want you to notice what's dominant 1st or where you sit. *"Always be happy to have other believers as visitors in your homes. God has helped each of you in a certain way. Think carefully about how to use that gift from God well. Remember that God has given his people many different gifts so they can help each other. Has God helped you to speak well? Then speak God's messages to people. Or has God helped you to serve other people? Then let God make you strong to do that. Do everything so that people will praise God. They will say that God is great because of Jesus Christ."* (1 Peter 4:9-11). Before you come up with your preplans, the area you're tied to may reveal some of these gifts. It's usually revealed through your talents and desires, separate from your spiritual gifts. Passions are much different from spiritual gifts, but you can start to locate gifts by looking up towards the lights.

Locate where you light up the most or where people are attracted to your light. Meaning it's some light peeking through the cracks of your life, and that's the area and starting point of recognizing your gifts. Just take your seat and look around you. Ask why people are calling upon you to do this or asking you to do that. Why is everyone looking up to you to lead, but you instead follow? This area is where your gift is tied too, and you need to discover this kind of flight. I discovered my wings, and I'll show you how I flew to this point.

Inside the church building was the environment of my discovery. I started to notice my functions through the steps of serving in the church. God commanded me to teach before I knew I had the ability. He told me to help my pastor, but that journey started with me standing up and clapping my hands. The more and more I got comfortable with myself, God noticed it and moved me to become an usher. I was challenged to speak throughout this season, and the teaching gift became evident to other church members. My light started to crack, and God positioned me in the space of an ordained deacon. By then, I became confident in my teaching abilities to lead the congregation in the word. One night I was trying to prepare a message and noticed a desire to write down everything in detail about what I wanted to teach. God then confirmed a message to me that if I recognize my fruit, I will recognize my power. In other words, writing down what I wanted to teach was discovering my ability to fly outside the home. My gift was tied to my church, and my wings were comfortable in the nest until God pushed me into the air. My altitude is the atmosphere of teaching the world about God through my own books now.

This is my space of rulership, but I also experienced turbulence while climbing through this environment. *"It is necessary to boast, though nothing is gained by it; but I will go on to visions and revelations of the Lord. I know a man in Christ who fourteen years ago- whether in the body I do not know, or out of the body I do not know, only God knows-such a man was caught up to the third heaven. And I know that such a man-whether in the body or out of the body, only God knows"* (2 Corinthians 2:1-3). In this passage, Paul spoke about having a transcendent experience where he was temporarily transported to a spiritual realm. My experience was similar; whether in the body or out, only

God knows. But what I do know was the spiritual speed bump I felt. One night, God decided to take me on a discovery flight at night. It had to be in the middle of the night, and I was lying in bed alone. Suddenly, I felt moved by force, like I was cocooned inside my body. But this push was powerful! Picture someone poking you to scoot over in bed, and you should understand this. This woke me up, but I couldn't move. The next thing I noticed was a presence around me, and I started levitating. This was a weird feeling, but in my Spirit, I quickly said, *"I want to go down."* Immediately, I became aware of my own body and the presence left. The whole time I was conscious of everything happening, but again, whether inside the body or not, I do not know; only God knows. The only thing I recognized was the safety of this presence. I didn't feel the presence of fear, so I knew it had to be God. This flight also consists of discerning spirits and prophecy, two of the spiritual gifts God gives. Discerning spirits is not only determining the true message of God vs. Satan; it's also being sensitive to the presence of spirits. Spirits operate in high places, and depending on your seat, you will encounter many of these winds, as my experience has shown you so far.

I never would've discovered any of this had I not taken these spiritual flights. I can't even see the destination in view, but I know where I started. Down there is where you started, but that's different from where you will end. You have a ticket to higher levels in heavenly places, and this ticket is seen through the invitations of the words of God. I was pushed out into the air to bring you up here to see yourself different from down there. But I've taken you as far as I can with my journey. Our journeys are different, and it's time for you to discover your wings and identify yourself.

I have some closing words from God that He needs you to hear, though. He says, *"I have poured my Spirit onto you and blessed you with gifts. You've been looking at yourself from a place of pain, regret, and emptiness for far too long. Make sure to distinguish what you did in the past from who you are now. Also, forgiving your parents would help because it's your time now. They didn't know who they were, but you're about to discover who you are. I'm speaking and calling forth the spirit man in you, the one I created, not the one the world formed. Please get to know that side of you now. I'm in your corner reminding you that I gave you power and authority; I promise never to leave or forsake you; If you submit to me, resist the devil, then he will flee from you; you are more than a conqueror; your flesh is weak, but your Spirit is ready. I need you to be bold and courageous because I wrote 66 books for you. Accept me as your savior and Spiritual Father, and walk in my footsteps. Your identity is high, and you will find it in ME!."*

Thank you for taking this time to read, and I hope I inspired you with some clarity. I pray that something I wrote freed you from any bondages. If it has, share your testimony with the world and praise Jesus Christ. I have more words to share with you, so keep in touch. Until the next time, remember I love you, and there's nothing you can do about it!